DYNAMITE RESUMES

Books by Drs. Ron and Caryl Krannich

The Almanac of American Government Jobs and Careers
The Almanac of International Jobs and Careers
Best Jobs For the 1990s and Into the 20th Century
Careering and Re-Careering For the 1990s
The Complete Guide to International Jobs and Careers
The Complete Guide to Public Employment
Discover the Right Job For You!
Dynamite Answers to Interview Questions
Dynamite Cover Letters
Dynamite Resumes
The Educator's Guide to Alternative Jobs and Careers
Find a Federal Job Fast!
High Impact Resumes and Letters
Interview For Success
Job Search Letters That Get Results
Jobs For People Who Love Travel
Mayors and Managers
Moving Out of Education
Moving Out of Government
Network Your Way to Job and Career Success
The Politics of Family Planning Policy
Re-Careering in Turbulent Times
Right SF-171 Writer
Salary Success
Shopping and Traveling in Exotic Asia
Shopping and Traveling in Exotic Hong Kong
Shopping and Traveling in Exotic Indonesia
Shopping and Traveling in Exotic Singapore and Malaysia
Shopping and Traveling in Exotic Thailand
Shopping and Traveling the Exotic Philippines
Shopping in Exciting Australia and Papua New Guinea
Shopping in Exotic Places
Shopping the Exotic South Pacific

DYNAMITE RESUMES

Ronald L. Krannich, Ph.D.
Caryl Rae Krannich, Ph.D.

IMPACT PUBLICATIONS
Woodbridge, VA

Dynamite Resumes

Library of Congress Cataloging-in-Publication Data

Krannich, Ronald L.
    Dynamite Resumes / Ronald L. Krannich, Caryl Rae Krannich.
      p. cm.
    Includes bibliographical references and index.
    ISBN 0-942710-52-5: $9.95.
    1. Resumes (Employment) I. Krannich, Caryl Rae. II. Title.
HF5383.K69   1992   91-40351
650.14—dc20   CIP

For information on distribution or quantity discount rates, call (703/361-7300), FAX (703/335-9486), or write to: Sales Department, IMPACT PUBLICATIONS, 4580 Sunshine Court, Woodbridge, VA 22192. Distributed to the trade by National Book Network, 4720 Boston Way, Suite A, Lanham, MD 20706, Tel. 301/459-8696.

CONTENTS

Chapter One

COMMUNICATE YOUR QUALIFICATIONS WITH POWER

When did you last write a dynamite resume? How well did you write, produce, distribute, and follow-up your resume? Who evaluated it and how? Did it immediately grab the attention of employers who called you for interviews? How well did it stand out from the crowd of other resumes? Did it clearly communicate your qualifications and future performance to potential employers? What did it really say about you as both a professional and a person? Did it become your ticket to job interviews or did it dash your job search expectations?

Regardless of what resulted from your previous resume efforts, let's turn to your future success which should include dynamite resumes.

YOU CAN DO BETTER

Resumes are some of the most abused and misused forms of job search communication. Not knowing how to best communicate their qualifications to employers, many job seekers go through the ritual of writing uninspired documents that primarily document their work history rather than provide evidence for predicting their future performance. Lacking a clear sense of purpose, they fail to properly connect their resume writing activities to their larger job search tasks. Rather than communicate their future performance to employers, they choose to document their past employment history which may or may not be relevant to employers' immediate and future needs.

But writing a resume is really the easiest step in the resume process. Once completing the writing exercise and producing it on attractive paper, many job seekers don't know how to best manage their resume in relation to potential employers. Most just send it in the mail as if job interviews and offers are primarily a function of increased direct-mail activity. Preoccupied with the magic of writing right, few job seekers engage in effective resume **distribution and follow-up** activities—the keys for getting your resume read and responded to. Instead, they circulate a lot of pretty paper that often goes to all the wrong places!

> *Preoccupied with the magic of writing right, few job seekers engage in effective resume distribution and follow-up activities.*

You can do better than most job seekers if you produce dynamite resumes. Unlike other resumes, dynamite resumes are designed with the larger job search in mind—they grab the attention of potential employers who, in turn, invite you to job interviews. You conduct dynamite interviews because your answers and questions are consistent with your dynamite resume. A dynamite resume is one that

- Clearly communicates a sense of purpose, professionalism, competence, honesty, enthusiasm, and likability.

- Consistently observes the rules of good resume writing—structure, form, grammar, word selection, categories, punctuation, spelling, inclusion/exclusion, length, graphics.

- Specifically links your interests, skills, abilities, and experience to the employer's present and future needs.

- Is produced in a professional manner, using the right combination of paper, ink, and equipment to further communicate your professional image.

- Gets distributed through the proper channels and delivered into the hands of the right people—those who make the hiring decision.

- Regularly gets followed-up with telephone calls, letters, and interviews.

Unlike many other resume books, which are primarily preoccupied with presenting proper resume form and content on paper, *Dynamite Resumes* focuses on the whole communication process, from producing an outstanding written document (form, content, and production elements) to distributing and following-up your resume with maximum impact. We focus on creating resumes that generate concrete **outcomes**—job interviews and offers.

A 30-SECOND IMAGE MANAGEMENT ACTIVITY

Resume writing is first and foremost a 30-second image management activity—it takes employers no more than 30 seconds to read and respond to your resume. Therefore, you must quickly **motivate** the reader to take action. Your resume must communicate your best professional image in writing **before** you can expect to be invited to a job interview. How and what you write, as well as which methods you choose to disseminate and follow-up your message, will largely determine how effective you are in moving the employer to take action in reference to your qualifications.

Keep in mind that most employers are busy people who must make quick judgments about you based upon your written message. Within only 30 seconds, your written communication must motivate the reader to either select you in or take you out of consideration for a job interview. Neglect the importance of a 30-second dynamite resume and you will surely neglect one of the most important elements in a successful job search. Your resume will join the graveyard of so many other ineffective resumes.

YOU ARE WHAT YOU WRITE

When writing and sending resumes to strangers, you essentially are what you write. Your one to two-page resume succinctly says a great deal about your professionalism, competence, and personality that goes beyond just documenting your work history, experience, and education. Your resume must have sufficient impact to move employers to contact you, interview you over the telephone, and hopefully invite you to a job interview that leads to a job offer and renewed career success. If you fail to properly write, produce, market, and follow-up your resume, you will most likely conduct an ineffective job search campaign.

RESUMES DO COUNT

Finding employment in today's job market poses numerous challenges for individuals who seek quality jobs that lead to good salaries, career advancement, and job security. The whole job finding process is chaotic, confusing, and frustrating. It requires a certain level of organization and communication skills aimed at identifying, contacting, and communicating your qualifications to potential employers. If you want to make this process best work for you, you must do more than just mail resumes in response to job vacancy announcements.

To be most successful in finding employment, you should develop a plan of action that involves these seven distinct yet interrelated job search steps:

1. Assess your skills

2. Develop a job/career objective

3. Conduct research on employers and organizations

4. Write resumes and letters

5. Network for information, advice, and referrals

6. Interview for jobs

7. Negotiate salary and terms of employment

As illustrated on page 6, each of these steps involves important **communication skills** involving you in contact with others. Assessing your skills (Step 1), for example, requires conducting a systematic assessment of what you do well and enjoy doing—your strengths or motivated abilities and skills (MAS) that become translated into your "qualifications" for employers. Conducting research on individuals, organizations, communities, and jobs (Step 4) requires the use of investigative skills commonly associated with library research. Networking and interviewing (Steps 5-6) primarily involve the use of conversational skills—small talk and structured question/answer dialogues —by telephone and in face-to-face encounters.

In the job search, paper is the great equalizer. Most employers want to see you on paper before meeting you in person.

But it is the critical resume and letter writing step (3) that becomes the major communication challenge for most job seekers. Without strong writing skills, your job search is likely to founder. Indeed, your ability to write dynamite resumes and cover letters largely determines how quickly you will transform your job search from the investigative stage (research) to employer contact stages (networking, interviewing, salary negotiations). Your writing skills become the key element in moving your job search from the investigative stage to the final job offer stage. Writing demonstrates your competence.

In the job search, paper is the great equalizer. Most employers want to first see you on paper before meeting you in person. You along with many

JOB SEARCH STEPS

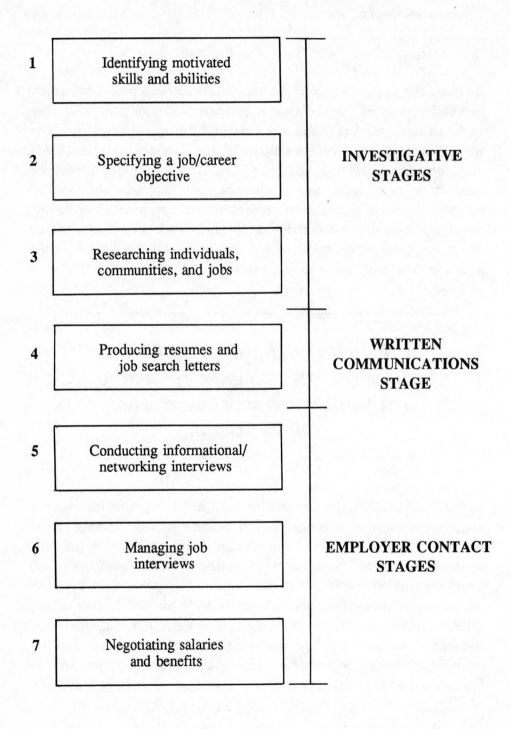

others must pass the written test **before** you can be considered for the face-to-face oral test. Whether you like it or not, you must put your professionalism, competence, and personality in writing before you can be taken seriously for a job interview. Thus, your writing activities may well become the most critical **transformation step** in your job search. Your writing skills become your ticket to job interviews that lead to job offers and employment.

For some reason job search writing skills usually receive little attention beyond the perfunctory *"you must write a resume and cover letter"* advisory. They also get dismissed as unimportant in a society that supposedly places its greatest value on telecommunicating and interpersonal skills. Indeed, during the past two decades many career advisors have emphasized networking as the key to getting a job; writing resumes and letters are considered relatively unimportant job search skills. Some even advise job seekers to dispense with the resume altogether and, instead, rely on cold-calling telephone techniques and "showing up" networking strategies.

But such advice is misplaced and misses one of the most important points in the job search. Resumes are an **accepted** means of communicating qualifications to employers. Indeed, employers expect to receive well-crafted resumes that represent the best professional efforts of candidates. The problem is that hiring officials receive so many poorly written and distributed resumes. Indeed, many candidates might be better off not writing a resume given the weaknesses they demonstrate by producing poorly constructed resumes. Failure to develop a well-crafted resume will disqualify you for many jobs. Resumes do not substitute for other equally important communication activities, but they do play a critical transformational role in your job search. They must be carefully linked to other key job search activities, especially networking and informational interviews which function as important **methods for disseminating resumes**.

You simply must write a resume if you are to be taken seriously in today's job market. And you will be taken most seriously if you write and disseminate dynamite resumes.

While some individuals do get interviews without writing resumes, you can do much better if you take the time and effort to develop a well-crafted resume and disseminate it properly. Your resume should focus on the employer's needs. It should demonstrate your professionalism, competence, and personality. Without an effective resume, your job search will have a limited impact on potential employers.

IMPROVE YOUR
JOB SEARCH EFFECTIVENESS

Just how effective are you in opening the doors of potential employers? Let's begin by identifying your level of job search information, skills, and strategies as well as those you need to develop and improve. You can do this by completing the following "job search competencies" exercise:

INSTRUCTIONS: Respond to each statement by circling which number at the right best represents your situation.

SCALE: 1 = strongly agree
              2 = agree
              3 = maybe, not certain
              4 = disagree
              5 = strongly disagree

1. I know what motivates me to excel at work.   1 2 3 4 5

2. I can identify my strongest abilities and skills.   1 2 3 4 5

3. I have at least seven major achievements that
    clarify a pattern of interests and abilities
    that are relevant to my job and career.   1 2 3 4 5

4. I know what I both like and dislike in work.   1 2 3 4 5

5. I know what I want to do during the next
    10 years.   1 2 3 4 5

6. I have a well defined career objective that
    focuses my job search on particular
    organizations and employers.   1 2 3 4 5

7. I know what skills I can offer employers in
    different occupations outside education.   1 2 3 4 5

8. I know what skills employers most seek in
    candidates.   1 2 3 4 5

9. I can clearly explain to employers what I
    do well and enjoy doing.   1 2 3 4 5

10. I can specify why employers should hire me.   1 2 3 4 5

11. I can gain support of family and friends
    for making a job or career change.   1 2 3 4 5

12. I can find 10 to 20 hours a week to
    conduct a part-time job search.   1 2 3 4 5

13. I have the financial ability to sustain
    a three-month job search.   1 2 3 4 5

14. I can conduct library and interview research
    on different occupations, employers,
    organizations, and communities.   1 2 3 4 5

15. I can write different types of effective
    resumes and job search/thank-you letters.   1 2 3 4 5

16. I can produce and distribute resumes and
    letters to the right people.   1 2 3 4 5

17. I can list my major accomplishments in
    action terms.   1 2 3 4 5

18. I can identify and target employers I
    want to interview with.   1 2 3 4 5

19. I can develop a job referral network.   1 2 3 4 5

20. I can persuade others to join in forming
    a job search support group.   1 2 3 4 5

21. I can prospect for job leads.   1 2 3 4 5

22. I can use the telephone to develop prospects
    and get referrals and interviews.   1 2 3 4 5

23. I can plan and implement an effective
    direct-mail job search campaign.   1 2 3 4 5

24. I can generate one job interview for every
    10 job search contacts I make.   1 2 3 4 5

25. I can follow-up on job interviews.   1 2 3 4 5

26. I can negotiate a salary 10-20% above
    what an employer initially offers.   1 2 3 4 5

27. I can persuade an employer to renegotiate
    my salary after six months on the job.   1 2 3 4 5

28. I can create a position for myself
    in an organization.   1 2 3 4 5

                                    TOTAL   _____

You can calculate your overall job search effectiveness by adding the numbers you circled for a composite score. If your total is more than 75 points, you need to work on developing your job search skills. How you scored each item will indicate to what degree you need to work on improving specific job search skills. If your score is under 50 points, you are well on your way toward job search success. In either case, this book should help you better focus your job search around the critical writing skills necessary for communicating your qualifications to employers. Other books can assist you with many other important aspects of your job search.

GET TAKEN
SERIOUSLY BY EMPLOYERS

The whole purpose of a job search is to get taken seriously by strangers who have the power to hire you. Your goal is to both discover and land a job you really want. You do this by locating potential employers and then persuading them to talk to you by telephone and in person about your interests and qualifications.

Being a stranger to most employers, you initially communicate your interests and qualifications on paper in the form of resumes and cover letters. How well you construct these documents will largely determine whether or not you will proceed to the next stage—the job interview.

The major weakness of job seekers is their inability to keep focused on their **purpose**. Engaging in a great deal of wishful thinking, they fail to organize their job search in a purposeful manner. They do silly things, ask dumb questions, and generally waste a great deal of time and money on needless activities. They frustrate themselves by going down the same deadend roads. Worst of all, they turn off employers by demonstrating poor communication skills, both written and oral.

The whole purpose of a job search is to be taken seriously by strangers who have the power to hire you.

The average job seeker often wanders aimlessly in the job market, as if finding a job were an ancient form of alchemy. Preoccupied with job search **techniques**, they lack an overall **purpose and strategy** that would give meaning and direction to discrete job search activities. They often engage in random and time-consuming activities that have little or no payoff. Participating in a highly ego-involved activity, they quickly lose sight of what's really important to conducting a successful job search—responding to the needs of employers. Not surprisingly, they aren't taken seriously by employers because they don't take themselves and the job search serious enough to organize their activities around key communication behaviors that persuade employers to invite them to job interviews. This should not happen to you.

The following pages are designed to increase your power to get taken seriously by employers. Individual chapters provide a quick primer on the key principles involved in writing, producing, evaluating, distributing, and following-up your own dynamite resume. It also presents numerous resume examples that illustrate the key principles involved in writing and revising dynamite resumes.

Since the examples in this book are presented to illustrate important resume writing **principles**, they should not be copied nor edited. As you will discover in the following pages, it is extremely important that you create your own resumes that express the "unique you" rather than send "canned" resumes to potential employers.

In the end, our goal is to improve your **communication effectiveness** in the job search. On completing this book, you should be able to write dynamite resumes that hopefully will result in many more invitations to job interviews.

DO WHAT'S EXPECTED
AND PRODUCES RESULTS

Based on experience, we assume most employers do indeed expect to receive well-crafted resumes. We proceed on the assumption that resumes are one of the most important elements in the job search.

The old interview adage that *"you never have a second chance to make a good first impression"* is equally valid for the resume. For it is usually the resume and cover letter rather than your telephone voice or appearance that first introduces you to a prospective employer. Your resume tells who you are and why an employer should want to spend valuable time meeting you in person. It invites the reader to focus attention on your key qualifications in relation to the employer's needs. It enables you to set an agenda for further exploring your interests and qualifications with employers.

Once you discover the importance of writing dynamite resumes, you will never again produce other types of resumes. Your dynamite resume will have the power to move you from stranger to interviewee to employee. It will open many more doors to job interviews and offers!

CHOOSE THE RIGHT RESOURCES

This book is primarily concerned with communicating your qualifications in writing to employers who, in turn, will be sufficiently motivated to invite you to a face-to-face job interview. Several of our other books deal with the key steps in the job search process as illustrated on page 6: *Careering and Re-Careering For the 1990s, Discover the Right Job For You!, High Impact Resumes and Letters, Dynamite Cover Letters, Interview For Success, Dynamite Answers To Interview Questions, Network Your Way To Job and Career Success*, and *Salary Success*. Others examine specific career fields, including government hiring processes, public employment strategies, the federal application form, and the special case of educators:

The Complete Guide To Public Employment, Find a Federal Job Fast!, The Almanac of American Government Jobs and Careers, The Right SF-171 Writer, and *The Educator's Guide To Alternative Jobs and Careers.* If your interests include the international employment arena, we have three books that can assist you: *The Complete Guide To International Jobs and Careers, The Almanac of International Jobs and Careers,* and *Jobs For People Who Love Travel.* For job alternatives, see our *Best Jobs For the 1990s and Into the 21st Century* and *Jobs and Careers With Nonprofit Organizations.* These and many other job search books are available directly from Impact Publications. For your convenience, you can order them by completing the form at the end of this book or by acquiring a copy of the publisher's catalog.

If you wish to acquire a copy of the most comprehensive career catalog available today—*"Jobs and Careers for the 1990s"*—which lists over 1,000 annotated job and career resources, write to:

> IMPACT PUBLICATIONS
> ATTN: Free Job/Career Catalog
> 4580 Sunshine Court
> Woodbridge, VA 22192

They will send you a free copy upon request. This catalog contains almost every important career and job finding resource available today, including many titles that are difficult, if not impossible, to find in bookstores and libraries. You will find everything from self-assessment books to books on resume writing, interviewing, government and international jobs, military, women, minorities, students, and entrepreneurs as well as videos and computer software programs. This is an excellent resource for keeping in touch with the major resources that can assist you with every stage of your job search as well as with your future career development plans.

PUT POWER INTO YOUR JOB SEARCH

Whatever you do, make sure you acquire, use, and taste the fruits of job search power. You should go into the job search equipped with the necessary knowledge and skills to be most effective in communicating your qualifications to employers.

As you will quickly discover, the job market is not a place to engage in wishful thinking. It's at times impersonal, frequently ego deflating, and often unforgiving of errors. It requires clear thinking, strong organizational skills, and effective strategies for making the right moves with employers. Above all, it rewards individuals who follow-through in implementing each job search step with enthusiasm, dogged persistence, and the ability to handle rejections.

May you soon discover this power and incorporate it in your own dynamite resume!

Chapter Two

RESUMES, READERS, MYTHS, AND MISTAKES

If you want your job search to be most effective, you must follow the principles of effective resume writing, production, distribution, and follow-up as well as regularly evaluate your progress. The principles range from obvious elementary concerns, such as correct spelling, punctuation, and placement of elements, to more complicated questions concerning when and how to best follow-up a resume mailed to an employer five days ago. Evaluation involves both internal self-evaluation mechanisms and external evaluators.

But before putting the principles and evaluations into practice, we need to examine the very concept of a resume within the larger job search. What exactly are we talking about? What is this thing called a resume and how does it relate to other steps in your job search? How do readers typically respond to resumes? What are some of the most common writing errors and mistakes one needs to avoid?

A great deal of mystery and confusion surrounds the purpose and content of resumes. Occupying a time-honored—almost ritual—place in the job finding process, resumes remain the single most important document you will write and distribute throughout your job search. Do it wrong and your job search will suffer accordingly. Do it right and your resume should give you the necessary entre for opening more doors to numerous job interviews and offers. The obvious choice is to write dynamite resumes for greater job search success.

YOUR RESUME HAS PURPOSE

What exactly is a resume? Is it a summary of your work history? An autobiography of your major accomplishments? A statement of your qualifications? A catalog of your interests, skills, and experience? An introduction to your professional and personal style? Your business calling card?

Let's be perfectly clear what we are talking about. A resume is all of these things and much much more. It is an important **product**—produced in reference to your goals, skills, and experience—that furthers two important **processes**—"job search" for you and "hiring" for employers. While it is a basic requirement when applying for many jobs, your resume plays a central role in directing you and your job search into productive information gathering and employment channels. It communicates your goals and capabilities to potential employers who must solve personnel problems— hire someone to perform particular functions and jobs. At the very least a resume represents the "unique you" to others who may or may not know much about your particular mix of goals and capabilities. It may represent the potential solution to employers' problems.

Better still, let's define a resume in terms of its **purpose** or **outcomes** for you in relation to hiring officials:

> ## A resume is an advertisement for an interview.

In other words, the purpose of writing, producing, distributing, and following-up a resume is to get job interviews—nothing more, nothing less. As such, your resume should follow certain principles of good advertising—grab attention, heighten interest, sell the product, and promote action. Your ultimate purpose in writing a resume is to **get employers to take action**—conduct a telephone interview as well as invite you to the first of several job interviews which will eventually result in job offers and employment. Thus, the purpose is a specific outcome.

If you define a resume in these terms, then the internal resume structure and specific elements included or excluded, as well as the production, distribution, and follow-up methods you choose, become self-evident. You should only include those elements that are of interest to employers. But what do they want to see? They simply want to see sound indicators of your **probable future performance** rather than a summary of your professional and personal history.

The logic here is very simple but needs repeating throughout your job search. Since employers will be hiring your future, they are more concerned with your future performance—*"What can you do for me?"*—rather than "the facts" about your past—*"Where did you go to school and what did you do during the summer of 1986?"* Therefore, you must present your past in such a manner that it clearly indicates **patterns of performance** that are good predictors of your future value and performance.

> *The purpose of writing, distributing, and following-up a resume is to get job interviews—nothing more, nothing less.*

KEEP FOCUSED ON EMPLOYERS' NEEDS

Without this central guiding purpose in mind, your resume is likely to take on a different form, as well as move in different directions, than outlined in this book. You simply must keep your resume writing, production, distribution, and follow-up activities focused around your purpose—

getting interviews. No distractions nor wishful thinking should interfere with this single-minded purpose.

Your approach, whether implicit or explicit, to resume writing says something about how you view yourself in relation to employers. It tells readers to what degree you are self-centered versus employer-centered. If you merely chronicle your past work history, you are likely to produce a self-centered resume that says little or nothing about your interests, skills, and abilities in relation to the employers' needs. Resumes lacking a central focus or purpose are good candidates for mindless direct-mail approaches— broadcasting them to hundreds of employers who by chance might be interested in your history.

On the other hand, if you thoughtfully develop a job objective that is sensitive to employers' performance needs and then relate your patterns of skills and accomplishments to that objective, you should produce a resume that transcends your history as it clearly communicates your qualifications to employers. This type of resume is **employer-centered**; it addresses employers' hiring needs. Such a resume is best targeted toward a select few employers who have job opportunities appropriate for your particular mix of interests, skills, and accomplishments. Therefore, the type of resume you produce tells employers a great deal about you both professionally and personally.

Your approach to resume writing says something about how you view yourself in relation to employers.

An intensely ego-involved activity, resume writing often goes awry as writers attempt to produce a document that he or she "feels good" about. Thinking a resume is analogous to an obituary, many writers believe their resume should summarize what's good about them. If the central purpose is to pile on a lot of good information about the individual's past, then a resume becomes a nonfocused dumping ground for a great deal of extraneous information employers neither need nor want. Such a resume may include lots of interesting facts that must be left to the interpretation of the reader who by definition is a very busy person; few such readers have the luxury of spending time analyzing and relating someone's chronicle of work history to their specific employment needs. Your resume may end up like most resumes—an uninspired listing of names, dates, and duties that are supposed to enlighten employers about your qualifications. While you may feel good writing such a document, don't expect employers to get excited enough to contact you for an interview. Your resume will likely end up in their "circular files", i.e., waste cans.

Always keep in mind your purpose: you are advertising yourself for a job interview.

Every time you make a decision concerning what to include or exclude in your resume and how and when to produce, distribute, and follow-up your job search communications, always keep in mind your purpose: you are advertising yourself for a job interview. This single-minded purpose will answer many questions you may have about the details of writing, producing, distributing, and following-up your resume. It will tell you what is and is not important in the whole resume writing, production, distribution, and follow-up process.

RESUME MYTHS AND REALITIES

Numerous myths about finding employment and contacting employers lead individuals down the wrong resume writing paths. The 10 most important myths and corresponding realities include these:

MYTH 1:   **The resume is the key to getting a job.**

REALITY: There is nothing magical about resumes. Indeed, there are many keys to getting a job, from being in the right place at the right time, having a good connection, to conducting an excellent job interview. The resume is only one step, albeit an important one, in the job finding process. Other steps depend on well-crafted resumes and cover letters. Remember, your resume is an advertisement for a job interview. Employers do not hire individuals because of the content or quality of their resume; the resume only gets them invited to job interviews. The job interview is the real key to getting the job; it is the prerequisite step for a job offer and employment contract. But you must first communicate your qualifications to employers through the medium of a top quality resume in order to get the job interview.

MYTH 2:   **The resume is not as important to getting a job as other job search activities such as networking and informational interviews.**

REALITY: Resumes still remain one of the most important written documents you will produce during your job search. If you expect to be interviewed for jobs, you simply must produce a well-crafted resume that clearly communicates your qualifications to employers. Whether you like it or not, employers want to see you on paper **before** talking to you over the telephone or seeing you in person. And they want to see a top quality resume—an attractive, error-free document that **represents your best self**. You should pay particular attention to the details and exacting quality required in producing a first-rate resume. Errors, however minor, can quickly eliminate you from consideration. Without such an error-free resume, you seriously limit your chances of getting job interviews. And without job interviews, you won't get job offers.

MYTH 3: It's best to send your resume to hundreds of employers rather than to just a few.

REALITY: Power in the job search comes from selective targeting—not through numbers. It comes from making a few contacts with the right people who have a specific **need** for your particular mix of interests, skills, and qualifications. While it may be comforting to think you are making progress with your job search by sending resumes to hundreds of potential employers, in reality you create an illusion of progress that will ultimately disappoint you; few people will seriously read an unsolicited resume and thus consider you for employment when they have no need. A resume broadcast or "shotgun" approach to finding a job indicates a failure to seriously focus your job search around the **needs** of specific employers. Your time, effort, and money will be better spent in marketing your resume in conjunction with other effective job search activities—networking and informational interview. These activities force you to concentrate on specific employers who would be most interested in your interests, skills, and qualifications. These individuals have a need that will most likely coincide with both your resume and job search timing.

Power in the job search comes from selective targeting.

MYTH 4: It's not necessary to include an objective.

REALITY: Without an objective your resume will lack a central focus from which to relate all other elements in your resume. An objective gives your resume organization and coherence. It tells potential employers that you are a **purposeful individual**—you have specific job and career goals in mind that are directly related to your past pattern of interests, skills, and experience as documented in the remainder of your resume. If properly stated, your objective will become the most powerful and effective statement on your resume. Without an objective, you force the employer to "interpret" your resume. He or she must analyze the discreet elements in each resume category and draw conclusions about your future capabilities which may or may not be valid. You force the person to engage in what may be a difficult analytical task, depending on their analytic capabilities. Therefore, it is to your advantage to control the flow and interpretation of your qualifications and capabilities by stating a clear employer-oriented objective. While you can state an objective in your cover letter, it is best to put your objective at the very beginning of your resume. After all, letters do get detached from resumes.

On the other hand, many people prefer excluding an objective because it tends to lock them into a particular type of job; they want to be flexible. Such people demonstrate a cardinal job search sin—they really don't know what they want to do; they tend to communicate their lack of focus in their resume as well as in other job search activities. They are more concerned with fitting into a job (*"Where are the jobs?"*) than with finding a job fit for them (*"Is this job right for me?"*)

MYTH 5: **The best type of resume outlines employment history by job titles, responsibilities, and inclusive employment dates.**

REALITY: This type of resume, the traditional chronological or "obituary" resume, may or may not be good for you. It's filled with historical "what" information—what work you did, in what organizations, over what period of time. Such resumes tell employers little about what it is you can do for them in the future. You should choose a resume format that clearly communicates your major strengths—not your history—to employers. Those strengths should be formulated as **patterns of performance** in relation to your goals and skills as well as the employer's needs. Your choice of formats include variations of the chronological, functional, and combination resumes—each offering different advantages and disadvantages, depending on your goals.

MYTH 6:   **Employers appreciate lengthy detailed resumes because they give them more complete information for screening candidates than shorter resumes.**

REALITY: Employers prefer receiving short, succinct one or two-page resumes. Longer resumes lose their interest and attention. Such resumes usually lack a focus, are filled with extraneous information, need editing, and are oriented toward your past rather than the employer's future. If you know how to write a dynamite resume, you can put all of your capabilities into a one to two-page format. These resumes only include enough information to persuade employers to contact you for an interview. Like good advertisements, they generate enough interest so the reader will contact you for more information (job interview) before investing in the product (job offer).

MYTH 7:   **It's okay to put salary expectations and references on your resume.**

REALITY: Two of the worst things you can do is to include salary information (history or expectations) and list your references on your resume. Remember, the purpose of your resume is to get an interview—nothing more, nothing less. Only during the interview—and preferably toward the end—should you discuss salary and share information on references. And before you discuss salary, you want to demonstrate your **value** to hiring officials as well as learn about the **worth** of the position. Only **after** you make your impression and gather information on the job, can you realistically talk about—and negotiate—salary. You can not do this if you prematurely mention salary on your resume.

Before you discuss salary you want to demonstrate your <u>value</u> to employers as well as learn about the <u>worth</u> of the position.

A similar principle applies to references. Never put your references on a resume. The closest you should ever get to mentioning names, addresses, and phone numbers—other than yours—is a simple statement appearing at the end of your resume:

"References available upon request"

You want to control your references for the interview. You should take a list of references appropriate for the position you will interview for with you to the interview. If you put references on your resume, the employer might call someone who has no idea you are applying for a particular job. The conversation could be embarrassing. As a simple courtesy, you need to ask your references ahead of time whether you may use their name as a reference. At that point, you want to brief your reference on the position you seek, explaining why you feel you should be selected by focusing on your goals and strengths in relation to the position. Give this person information that will support your candidacy. Surprisingly, though, few employers actually follow-through by contacting stated references! This is perhaps one reason they often make poor hiring decisions. Many employers are surprised to later discover a problem employee had similar problems in previous jobs.

MYTH 8: **You should not include your hobbies nor any personal statements on a your resume.**

REALITY: In general this is true. However, there are exceptions which would challenge this rule as a myth. If you have a hobby or a personal statement that can strengthen your objective in relation to the employer's needs, consider including it on your resume. For example, if a job calls for someone who is outgoing and energetic, you would not want to include a hobby or personal statement that indicates that you are a very private and sedentary person, such as *"enjoy reading and writing"* or *"collect stamps."* But *"enjoy organizing community fund drives"* and *"compete in the Boston Marathon"* might be very appropriate statements for your resume. Such statements further emphasize the "unique you" in relation to your capabilities, the requirements for the position, and the employer's needs.

MYTH 9: **You should try to get as much as possible on each page of your resume.**

REALITY: Each page of your resume should be appealing to the eye. It should make an immediate favorable impression, be inviting and easy to read, and look professional. You achieve these qualities by using a variety of layout, type style, highlighting, and emphasizing techniques. When formatting each section of your resume, be sure to make generous use of white space. Bullet, underline, or bold items for emphasis. If you try to cram a great deal on each page, your resume will look cluttered and uninviting to the reader. You may make just the opposite impression you thought you were making in an ostensibly well organized resume—you look disorganized!

MYTH 10: **Once you send your resume to an employer, there's nothing you can do except wait for a reply.**

REALITY: Waiting for potential employers to contact you is not a good job search strategy. Sending a resume to a potential employer is only the first step in connecting with a potential job. You should always **follow-up** your resume with a phone call, preferably within seven days, to answer questions, conduct a telephone interview, get invited to a job interview, or acquire additional information, advice, and referrals. Without this follow-up action, your resume is likely to get lost amongst many other resumes that compete for the reader's attention.

Taken together, these myths and realities emphasize one overriding concern when writing a resume:

> **The key to effective resume writing is to give the reader, within the space of one to two pages, just enough interesting information about your past performance and future capabilities so he or she will get sufficiently excited to contact you for a job interview.**

It is during the interview, rather than on your resume, that you will provide detailed answers to the most important questions concerning the job. Those questions are determined by both the interviewer and you during the job interview. Don't prematurely eliminate yourself from consideration by including too much or too little information, or being too boastful or too negative, on your resume before you get to the interview stage. In this sense, your resume becomes an important "window of opportunity" to get invited to job interviews that hopefully will translate into good job offers.

COMMON WRITING ERRORS AND MISTAKES

A resume must first get written and written well. And it is at the initial writing stage that many deadly errors and mistakes get made. The most common errors occur when writers fail to keep the purpose of their resume in mind.

Most errors kill a resume even before it gets fully read.

Most errors kill a resume even before it gets fully read. At best these errors leave negative impressions which are difficult to overcome at this or any other point in the hiring process. Remember, hiring officials have two major inclusion/exclusion concerns in mind when reading your resume:

- They are looking for excuses to eliminate you from further consideration.

- They are looking for evidence to consider you for a job interview.

Every time you make an error, you provide supports for eliminating you from further consideration. Concentrate, instead, on providing supports for being considered for a job interview.

Make sure your resume is not "dead on arrival." To insure against this, avoid the most common errors reported by employers who regularly review resumes:

- **NOT RELATED TO THE READER'S INTERESTS OR NEEDS.** Not another one of these! Why was this sent to me? I don't have a job vacancy nor do we perform work related to this person's skills. Did they purchase someone's mailing list? They need to take their job search seriously by being more informed about employers and organizations before sending out such junk mail. In the meantime, this person has just wasted my time, which is both limited and precious to me. I hope they don't plan to further waste my time by following-up their resume and letter with a phone call!

- **TOO LONG, SHORT, OR CONDENSED.** Ugh! What a waste of time and effort. Don't they have a better sense of self-esteem?

- **POOR FORMAT AND PHYSICAL APPEARANCE.** This person probably doesn't look any better than her paper presentation. I have a bad feeling about this person. I've met this type before—really boring people.

- **MISSPELLINGS, BAD GRAMMAR, AND WORDINESS.** When will they learn to write a simple sentence that conveys a basic level of literacy? I wonder what other communication problems this person brings to the job? These errors are insulting. I really don't need this trouble.

- **POOR PUNCTUATION.** I wonder how much training this person will need to get up to speed? This could be an expensive hire—and fire!

- **LENGTHY PHRASES, SENTENCES, AND PARAGRAPHS.** The language here is English. I wonder where they learned to do this? Maybe they talk the same way—on and on and on.

- **TOO SLICK, AMATEURISH, AND "GIMMICKY."** I'm impressed. Yeah, I bet this person is the hottest thing since sliced bread. Just what I need—a manipulator on the payroll. I don't need gimmicks—only an enthusiastic individual who has a solid and predictable pattern of performance.

- **TOO BOASTFUL OR DISHONEST.** I've seen this before. This one's too hot to handle—I'll regret the day I contacted him for an interview.

- **POORLY TYPED AND REPRODUCED.** Isn't this nice. I'm really impressed with the quality of this individual. Maybe I'm not important enough to receive a better quality resume.

- **IRRELEVANT INFORMATION.** Do I really need to know your height, weight, number of children, and spouse's name? I wonder what other irrelevances this person can bring to the interview, and the job. Don't they know what I need?

- **CRITICAL CATEGORIES MISSING.** Where's the objective? Where did she work? Any special awards, recognitions, accomplishments? What about education? What years did this include?

- **HARD TO UNDERSTAND OR REQUIRES TOO MUCH INTERPRETATION.** I really don't have time to do a content analysis of this individual's skills and accomplishments. After reading two pages of "bio facts," I still don't know what this person can do. He did a great deal, but I can't tell what he's really good at doing other than a lot of different jobs.

- **UNEXPLAINED TIME GAPS.** What did he do between 1984 and 1987? Unemployed? Trying to find himself abroad? In school? A drug or criminal problem?

- **DOES NOT CONVEY ACCOMPLISHMENTS OR A PATTERN OF PERFORMANCE FROM WHICH THE READER CAN PREDICT FUTURE PERFORMANCE.** This is all interesting, but what can the person do for me? I want to be able to predict what this person will likely do in my organization.

- **TEXT DOES NOT SUPPORT OBJECTIVE.** Nicely stated objective, but there's no evidence this person has any experience or skills in line with the objective. Could this be a statement of "wishful thinking" or something that has been "boiler plated" from someone else's resume?

- **UNCLEAR OR VAGUE OBJECTIVE.** What exactly does this person want to do career-wise as well as in my organization? Perhaps this person really doesn't know what he wants to do other than get a good paying job.

- **LACKS CREDIBILITY AND CONTENT—INCLUDES LOTS OF FLUFF AND "CANNED" RESUME LANGUAGE.** Where do they get all this dreadful stuff? Probably using the same old resume writing book that emphasizes action verbs and transferable skills but fails to advise them to include some content. Where's the beef?

This listing of writing errors and possible reader responses emphasizes how important **both** form and content are when writing a resume with purpose. You must select an important form, arrange each element in an attractive manner, and provide the necessary substance to grab the attention of the reader and move him or her to action. And all these elements of good resume writing must be related to the needs of your audience. If not, you may quickly kill your resume by committing some of these deadly errors.

Remember, hiring officials are busy people who only devote a few seconds to reading your resume. They are seasoned at identifying errors that will effectively remove you from further consideration. They want to see you error-free on paper so they can concentrate on what they need to do—evaluate your qualifications for employment.

QUALITIES OF EFFECTIVE RESUMES

A well-crafted resume expresses many important professional and personal qualities employers seek in candidates:

- Your **level of literacy**.

- Your **ability to conceptualize and analyze** your own interests, skills, and abilities in relation to the employer's needs.

- Your **patterns of performance**.

- Your ability to clearly communicate **who you are** and **what you want to do** rather than who you have been and what you have done.

- Your **view of the employer**—how important he is in relation to your interests, skills, and abilities.

These qualities are expressed through certain resume principles which you can learn and apply to most employment situations. Your resume should

- Immediately impress the reader.

- Be visually appealing and easy-to-read

- Indicate your career aspirations and goals.

- Focus on employers' needs.

- Communicate your job-related **abilities** and **patterns of performance**—not past or present job duties and responsibilities.

- Stress your productivity in terms of your potential for solving employers' problems.

- Communicate that you are a responsible and purposeful person who gets things done.

If you keep these general principles in mind, you should be able to produce a dynamite resume that will grab the attention of employers who will be moved to action—invite you to a job interview. To do less is to communicate the wrong messages to employers—you lack purpose, literacy, good judgment, and a pattern of performance.

ALWAYS REMEMBER YOUR AUDIENCE AND YOUR PURPOSE

When deciding what to include in your resume, always remember these important writing guidelines for creating a dynamite resume:

1. View your resume as your personal **advertisement**.

2. Focus on the purpose of your resume which is to get a **job interview**.

3. Take the offensive by developing a resume that **structures the reader's thinking** around your objective, qualifications, strengths, and projections of future performance.

4. Make your resume **generate positive thinking** rather than raise negative questions or confuse readers.

5. Focus your resume on the **needs of your audience**.

6. Communicate clearly what it is you **want to do and can do** for the reader.

7. Always be **honest** without being stupid. Stress your positives; never volunteer nor confess your negatives.

If you keep these basic purposes and principles in mind, you should produce a dynamite resume as well as conduct a job search that is both purposeful and positive. Your resume should stand out above the crowd as you clearly communicate your qualifications to employers.

In the next two chapters we'll take an in-depth look at these and several other principles relevant to the whole spectrum of resume activities—writing, producing, distributing, following-up, and evaluating.

Chapter Three

61 WRITING, PRODUCTION, DISTRIBUTION, AND FOLLOW-UP PRINCIPLES

Effective resumes follow certain writing, production, distribution, and follow-up principles that are specific to the resume medium and relevant to the job search process. These principles should be incorporated into every stage of the resume writing, production, distribution, and follow-up process.

WRITING

Overall Strategy

1.   **DO FIRST THINGS FIRST IN MAKING YOUR RESUME REPRESENT THE "UNIQUE YOU":** Avoid creatively plagiarizing others' resumes, however tempting and easy to do. A widely abused approach to resume writing, creative plagiarizing occurs when someone decides to take shortcuts by writing their resume in reference to so-called "outstanding resume examples"; they basically edit the examples by substituting information on themselves for what appears in the example. The result is a

resume filled with a great deal of "canned" resume language that
may be unrelated to the individual's goals, skills, and experience.

Do first things first by starting with a self-assessment that will help you build each section of your resume.

The best resumes are those based on a thorough self-assessment
of your interests, skills, and abilities which, in turn, is the **foundation** for stating a powerful objective, shaping information in each
category, and selecting proper resume language. What, for
example, do you want to do before you die? Answering this
question in detail will tell you a great deal about your values and
goals in relation to your career objectives. You may want to
incorporate this information into your resume. Do first things first
by starting with a self-assessment that will help you build each
section of your resume. Numerous exercises and instruments are
available for conducting your own self-directed assessment of
your interests, skills, and abilities. These are outlined in several
other career planning and job search books we and others have
written. Several are identified in the "Career Resources" section
at the very end of this book (pages 152-154). Professional testing
centers and career counselors also administer a variety of useful
self-assessment devices. Information on such services is readily
available through your local community college, adult education
programs, or employment services office.

2.   **DEVELOP A PLAN OF ACTION RELEVANT TO YOUR
     OVERALL JOB SEARCH:** Make sure your resume is part of
     your larger job search plan. In addition to incorporating self-
     assessment data, it should be developed with specific goals in
     mind, based on research, and related to networking and informa-

tional interviewing activities. Begin by asking yourself broader *"What do I want to do with this resume?"* question rather than narrow your focus on the traditional *"What should I include on my resume?"* question.

Structure and Organization

3. **SELECT AN APPROPRIATE RESUME FORMAT THAT BEST COMMUNICATES YOUR GOALS, SKILLS, EXPERI-ENCE, AND PREDICTED FUTURE PERFORMANCE:** Resume format determines how you organize the information categories for communicating your qualifications to employers. It **structures the reader's thinking** about your goals, strengths, and probably future performance. If, for example, your basic organization principle is chronology (dates you worked for different employers), then you want employers to think of your qualifications in historical terms and thus deduce future performance based upon an analysis of performance **patterns** evidenced in your work history. If your basic organizational principle is skills, then you want employers to think of you in achievement terms.

   You essentially have three formats from which to choose: chronological, functional, or combination. A **chronological re-sume**—often referred to as an "obituary resume"—is the most popular resume format but it is by no means the most appropriate. Primarily summarizing work history, this resume lists dates and names of employers first and your duties and responsibilities second. It often includes a great deal of extraneous information. In its worst form—the traditional chronological resume—it tells employers little or nothing about what you want to do, can do, and will do for them. In its best form—the improved chronological resume—it communicates your purpose, past achievements, and probable future performance to employers. It includes an objective which relates to other elements in the resume. The work experience section includes names and addresses of former employers followed by a brief description of accomplishments, skills, and responsibilities rather than formal duties and responsi-bilities; inclusive employment dates appear at the end. Chronological resumes should be used by individuals who have a progressive record of work experience and who wish to advance within an occupational field. One major advantage of these resumes is that they include "the beef" employers wish to see.

Functional resumes emphasize patterns of skills and accomplishments rather than job titles, employers, and inclusive employment dates. These resumes should be used by individuals making a significant career change, first entering the work force, or re-entering the job market after a lengthy absence. Since many employers still look for names, dates, and direct work experience—the so-called "beef"—this type of resume often disappoints employers who are looking for more substantive information relating to "experience" and "qualifications." You should use a functional resume only if your past work experience does not clearly support your objective.

Combination resumes combine the best elements of chronological and functional resumes. They stress patterns of accomplishments and skills as well as include work history. Work history appears as a separate section immediately following the presentation of accomplishments and skills in an "Areas of Effectiveness" or "Experience" section. This is the perfect resume for individuals with work experience who wish to change to a job in a related career field.

Examples of these different types of resumes are included in the remainder of this book. They are illustrated in the resume transformations found in Chapter Five.

4. **INCLUDE ALL ESSENTIAL INFORMATION CATEGORIES IN THE PROPER ORDER:** What you should or should not include in your resume depends on your particular goals as well as your situation and the needs of your audience. When deciding on what to include, always keep in mind the **needs** of the employer. What does he or she want or need to know about you? The most important information relates to your **future performance** which is normally determined by assessing your **past patterns of performance** ("experience" presented as "accomplishments," "outcomes," "benefits," or "performance"). At

the very least your resume should include the following five categories of information which help provide answers to five major questions:

Information category	**Relevant question**
Contact information	Who you are/how to contact you.
Objective	What you **want to do.**
Experience	What you **can do**—your patterns of skills and accomplishments.
Work history	What you **have done.**
Educational background	What you **have learned.**

Taken together, these information categories and corresponding questions provide evidence for answering a sixth unanswered question:

What you will most likely do in the future.

Finding answers to this implicit question is the employer's ultimate goal in the hiring process. Employers must deduce the answer from examining what you said in each category of your one to two-page resume. Employers must make an important **judgment** about your future performance **with them** by carefully considering what you want to do (your objective), what you can do (your experience), and what you have done and learned (your work history and education). A resume incorporating only these five categories of information should be sufficiently powerful to answer most employers' critical questions.

Other information categories often found on resumes include the following:

- Military experience
- Community involvement
- Professional affiliations

- Special skills
- Interests and activities
- Personal statement

The most important information relates to your <u>future performance</u> which is normally determined by assessing your <u>past patterns of performance</u>.

---

5. **SEQUENCE THE CATEGORIES ACCORDING TO THE PRINCIPLE OF WHAT'S MOST IMPORTANT TO BOTH YOU AND THE EMPLOYER:** You want your most important information and your strongest qualifications to always come first. Recent graduates with little or no relevant work experience, for example, should put education first since it's probably their most important "qualification" at this stage of their worklife. Your educational experience tells employers what you may have learned and thus provides some evidence of a certain knowledge, skill, and motivational base from which you possess a **capacity** to learn and grow within the employer's organization, i.e., you are functionally trainable. Your education also may include important work experience and achievements that indicate a pattern of future performance. Education should also come first in cases where education is an important **qualifying criteria**, especially for individuals with professional degrees and certifications: teachers, professors, doctors, nurses, lawyers, accountants, counselors. Recent graduates with little or no work experience may also want to put education first. The sequence of elements should be

    - Contact information
    - Education
    - Experience
    - Work history

Students or others with little or no work history should omit the "Work history" category (putting little or no information here can be a negative) but convert "Experience" into a new and expanded category: "Areas of Effectiveness" or "Capabilities." This section becomes the central focus that defines a functional resume.

If you have a few or several years of direct work experience that supports your objective, and if education is not an important qualifying criteria, then your "Experience" section should immediately follow your objective. In this case "Education" moves toward the end of the resume:

- Contact information
- Experience
- Work history
- Education

Any other categories of information should appear either immediately after "Work history" or after "Education."

6. **AVOID INCLUDING EXTRANEOUS INFORMATION UN-RELATED TO YOUR OBJECTIVE AND THE NEEDS OF EMPLOYERS:** However ego-involved you become in the resume writing process, always remember your goal and your audience. You are writing to a potential employer who by definition is a critical stranger who has specific needs. You are not writing to your mother, spouse, lover, friends, or former teachers. The following extraneous information often appears on resumes:

- **The word "RESUME" at the top:** The reader already knows this is your resume, assuming you have chosen a standard resume format. It's not necessary to label it as such.

- **Present date:** This goes on your cover letter rather than your resume.

- **Picture:** Include a picture only if it is essential for a job, such as in modeling or theater. A picture may indeed be worth "a thousand words," but 990 of those words you don't need distracting from the central focus of your resume! Concentrate instead on the words and information **you** can control.

- **Race, religion, or political affiliation:** Include this information only if these are bona-fide occupational qualifications, which they should not be given current anti-discrimination and equal opportunity laws.

- **Salary history or requirements:** Never ever include salary history or expectations on your resume. If you are forced to submit this information at the initial screening stage, do so in your cover letter. Salary usually is negotiable. The salary question should only arise at the end of the interview or during the job offer—after you have had a chance to assess the worth of the job as well as demonstrate your value to hiring officials. It should not arise prematurely on a resume.

- **References:** Always make your references "available upon request." You want to control the selection of references as well as alert your references that you are applying for a specific position and that they may be contacted.

- **Personal information such as height, weight, age, sex, marital status, health:** Few, if any, of these characteristics strengthen or relate to your objective. Many are negatives. Some could be positives, but only if you are a model, karate instructor, or applying for a position which views these as bona-fide occupational qualifications.

- **Any negative information:** Employment gaps, medical or mental problems, criminal records, divorces, terminations, conflicting interests. There is absolutely no reason for you to volunteer potential negatives on your resume. This is the quickest way to get eliminated from consideration. Always remember that your resume should represent your very "best self." If hiring officials are interested in learning about your negatives, they will ask you and you should be prepared to respond in a positive manner—but only at the interview stage.

Since most of this extraneous information is a real negative in the eyes of employers—and has little to do with your supporting your objective as well as answering employers' six critical questions—avoid including this information on your resume.

Contact Information

7. **PUT ALL ESSENTIAL CONTACT INFORMATION AT THE VERY TOP OF YOUR RESUME AS THE HEADER:** The very first element a reader should see on your resume is an attractive header. At a minimum this includes your name, address, and phone number displayed in one of several alternative layouts:

JAMES LAWSON
8891 S. Hayward Blvd.
Buffalo, NY 14444
Tel. 707/321-9721

JAMES LAWSON

8891 S. Hayward Blvd.   Buffalo, NY 14444   Tel. 707/321-9721

JAMES LAWSON

8891 S. Hayward Blvd.   Tel. 707/321-9721
Buffalo, NY 14444

JAMES LAWSON

8891 S. Hayward Blvd.   Buffalo, NY 14444   Tel. 707/321-9721

JAMES LAWSON
8891 S. Hayward Blvd.
Buffalo, NY 14444   Tel. 707/321-9721

We prefer capitalizing the name, although using upper and lower case letters is fine. We also prefer the first header because it introduces a very neat, clean, and eye-pleasing resume layout which is very inviting to readers who quickly survey resumes. We use this format extensively in the examples throughout this book.

Avoid using P.O. Box numbers; they communicate the wrong message about your housing situation.

---

8.   **INCLUDE YOUR COMPLETE CONTACT INFORMATION:** Employers want to know how to contact you immediately should they have any questions or wish to invite you to an interview. Therefore, only include information which enables the employer to make such a quick contact. Be sure to include **complete** contact information—name, address, and phone number. Avoid using P.O. Box numbers; they communicate the wrong message about your housing situation—you do not have a stable address. Also, include

a daytime telephone number through which you can be reached. If you do not have a telephone, or if your only daytime number is with your present employer, enlist a telephone answering service or use someone else's number who will be available and willing to screen your calls. They, in turn, can contact you at work and then you can return the call. Include your first and last name, and maybe your middle initial, depending on your professional style. The use of a middle initial is the sign of greater formality and is most frequently used by established professionals. However, using your full first, middle, and last name together is too formal: ROBERT DAVID ALLAN. If you prefer using your middle name rather than first name, do so either alone or in combination with your first initial: ROBERT ALLAN or J. ROBERT ALLAN. Do not include nick names (ROBERT "BUDZY" ALLAN) unless you feel it will somehow help your candidacy, which it most likely will not! Include any professional titles, such as M.D., Ph.D., J.D., immediately after your last name: ROBERT ALLAN, J.D. Never begin your name with a formal gender designation: Mr., Mrs., or Ms. Your address should be complete, including a zip code number. It's okay to abbreviate the state (NY for New York, IL for Illinois, CA for California) as well as certain common locational designations: N. for North, SW for Southwest, Ave. for Avenue, St. for Street, Blvd. for Boulevard, Apt. for Apartment. However, it's best to spell out Circle, Terrace, or Lane. Be sure to include your telephone number; you may want to preface it with "Tel." or "Tel:". If you have a fax number, you may want to include it immediately following your telephone number:

        Tel. 819/666-2197
        Fax 819/666-2222

If you are applying for a position abroad, try to include a fax number. Do not clutter your header with extraneous information, such as age, marital status, sex, height, and weight. Such information is totally irrelevant—indeed a negative—on a resume. It communicates the wrong messages and indicates you don't know how to properly present yourself to potential employers. These are not qualifying criteria for most jobs. Such information should never be volunteered during your job search. Moreover, most is illegal information for employers to elicit from candidates.

Objective

9. **INCLUDE A JOB OR CAREER OBJECTIVE RELEVANT TO YOUR SKILLS, EMPLOYERS' NEEDS, AND THE REMAINING ELEMENTS OF YOUR RESUME:** While some resume advisors consider an objective to be an optional item—preferring to keep it general or place it in a cover letter—or provide little guidance on how to structure an objective and relate it to other resume elements, we strongly recommend including a powerful objective at the very beginning of your resume. Your objective should be the **central organizing element** from which all other elements in your resume flow. It should tell employers what it is you **want to do**, **can do**, and **will do** for them.

Your objective should be employer-centered rather than self-centered.

Put in its most powerful form, your objective should be employer-centered rather than self-centered. It should incorporate both a skill and an outcome in reference to your major strengths and employer's major needs. Rather than being a statement of wishful thinking ("A position in management") or opportunistic ("A research position with opportunity for career advancement"), it should focus on your major strengths **in relation to** an employer's needs. Take, for example, the following objective statement:

"A position in data analysis where skills in mathematics, computer programming, and deductive reasoning will contribute to new systems development."

This type of objective follows a basic **job—skill—benefit** format:

"I want a _____ where I will use my
              position/job

_____ which will result in
  skills and abilities to

_____."
  outcomes and benefits

Restated in this basic format, the above objective would appear in this form:

"A <u>data analysis job</u> where I will use my <u>skills in mathematics, computer programming, and deductive reasoning</u> which will result in <u>new systems development</u>.

An objective based on this originating statement follows a very specific form. The first part of this objective statement emphasizes a specific position in relation to your strongest skills or abilities; the second part relates your skills to the employer's needs. Such an objective becomes a statement of **benefits** employers can expect from you. All other elements in your resume (experience, work history, education, awards) should provide **supports** for your objective. Formulated in this manner, your objective becomes the most important element on your resume as well as in your job search; it directs all other elements appearing on your resume, determining what should or should not be included in each section. It also gives your job search direction, focusing your efforts toward particular employers and helps you formulate well focused answers to interview questions. While formulating such an objective may be very time consuming—your two to three-line objective statement may take several days to develop and refine—the end result will be a well-focused resume that communicates your value and benefits to employers.

10. **AN OBJECTIVE SHOULD BE NEITHER TOO GENERAL NOR TOO SPECIFIC:** Many resume writers prefer developing a very general objective so their resume can be used for many different types of jobs. However, highly generalized objectives often sound "canned" or are meaningless (*"A position working with people that leads to career advancement"*); they may indicate you don't know what you really want to do. Indeed, if your purpose is to apply for many different types of jobs, you are attempting to fit into jobs rather than find jobs fit for you. You appear to lack a clear focus on what you want to do. On the other hand, a very specific objective may be too narrow for most jobs; you may appear too specialized for many positions. Another alternative is to write a separate or targeted objective, responsive to the requirements of each position, every time you send a resume to a hiring official. This approach should result in resumes that are most responsive to the needs of individual employers. However, you may have difficulty doing this unless you have word processing capabilities that allow you to custom-design each resume. An objective that is not too general nor too specific will serve you well for most resume occasions. It should indicate you know exactly what you want to do without being overly specific. Look at our examples in chapters Five and Six for objectives that are neither too general nor too specific.

11. **RELATE ALL OTHER RESUME ELEMENTS TO YOUR OBJECTIVE, EMPHASIZING SKILLS, OUTCOMES, AND BENEFITS:** All other elements appearing on your resume should reinforce your objective. When deciding what to include or exclude on your resume, ask yourself this question: *"Will this information strengthen my objective, which emphasizes my skills in relation to the employer's needs?"* If the answer is *"yes,"* include it. If the answer is *"no,"* exclude it. Remember, the most effective one to two-page resume clearly and concisely communicates your objectives and strengths to employers. If you fail to organize your resume in this manner, you are likely to include a great deal of extraneous information that communicates the wrong message to employers—you don't know what you want to do;

your interests, skills, and experience are peripheral or unrelated to the reader's needs; your lack a clear focus and thus appear disorganized. These are cardinal sins committed by many resume writers who produce self-centered resumes that fail to respond to the needs of employers. Make sure each section of your resume clearly and consistently communicates what it is you **want to do**, **can do**, and **will do** for employers.

Summary of Qualifications

12. **YOU MAY WANT TO INCLUDE A "SUMMARY OF QUALIFICATIONS" SECTION IMMEDIATELY FOLLOWING YOUR "OBJECTIVE":** Some resume writers prefer including a short one-line objective but immediately following it with a three or four-line "Summary of Qualifications" statement. This statement attempts to crystalize the individual's major strengths that are also relevant to the objective. It is usually a synthesis of the "Experience" section. We consider this an optional item to be used by individuals with a great deal of work experience and who choose a chronological resume format. It is most effective on chronological resumes where the objective is weak and the experience sections are organized by position, organization, and inclusive employment dates. The "Summary of Qualifications" section enables you to synthesize in capsule form your most important skills and accomplishments as patterns of performance. Especially with chronological resumes, this can be a very effective section. It helps elevate your resume by stressing major accomplishments and thus overcoming the inherent limitations of chronological resumes. An example of such a statement includes the following:

SUMMARY OF QUALIFICATIONS

Twelve years of progressively responsible experience in all phases of retail sales and marketing with major discount stores in culturally diverse metropolitan areas. Annually improved profitability by 15 percent and consistently rated in top 10 percent of workforce.

As noted in our example of Mark Able in Chapter Six, the remainder of this resume provides supports for this statement in the "Experience" section.

Work Experience

13. **ELABORATE YOUR WORK EXPERIENCE IN DETAIL WITH PARTICULAR EMPHASIS ON YOUR SKILLS, ABILITIES, AND ACHIEVEMENTS:** Next to your objective, your work experience section will be the most important. Here you need to give the details on your past accomplishments. To best develop this section, complete worksheets which include the following information on each job:

    ■ Name of employer
    ■ Address
    ■ Inclusive employment dates
    ■ Type of organization
    ■ Size of organization/number of employees
    ■ Approximate annual sales volume or annual budget
    ■ Position held
    ■ Earnings per month/year
    ■ Responsibilities/duties
    ■ Achievements or significant contributions
    ■ Demonstrated skills and abilities
    ■ Reason(s) for leaving

    We include several worksheets for generating this information in the Appendix on pages 141-148. It's best to complete these worksheets **before** starting to write your resume.

14. **KEEP EACH "EXPERIENCE" SECTION SHORT AND TO THE POINT:** Information for each job should be condensed into descriptions of five to eight lines. The language should be crisp, succinct, expressive, and direct. Keep editing—eliminate unnecessary words and phrases—until you have short, succinct, and powerful statements that grab the attention of the reader. Lengthy

statements tend to lose the reader's attention and distract from your major points. The guiding principle here is to edit, edit, edit, and edit until you get it right!

Edit, edit, edit, and edit until you get it right!

---

15. **WORK EXPERIENCE SHOULD BE PRESENTED IN THE LANGUAGE OF SKILLS AND ACCOMPLISHMENTS RATHER THAN FORMAL DUTIES AND RESPONSIBILITIES:** Employers are not interested in learning about duties and responsibilities assigned to your previous jobs which are essentially a rehash of your formal job descriptions. These come with the position regardless of who occupies the position. Instead, potential employers want to know how well you performed your assigned duties and responsibilities as well as any additional initiative you took that produced positive results. Since they are looking for indicators of your performance, it's to your advantage to describe your previous jobs in performance terms—what skills you used, what resulted from your work, and how your employer benefitted. These are usually termed your "accomplishments" or "achievements." An accomplishment or achievement is anything you did well that resulted in a positive outcome. Accomplishments are what define your "patterns of performance." Rather than state that your

> Responsibilities included conducting research projects assigned to office and coordinating projects with three research and development offices. Duties also involved evaluating new employees and chairing monthly review meetings.

Restate this "work experience" in terms of your actual accomplishments or achievements:

Conducted research on transportation of hazardous wastes on interstate highways which provided the basis for new restrictive legislation (PL4921). Developed three proposals for studying the effects of toxic waste dumps on rural water supplies which received $1.75 million in funds. Chaired interdepartmental meetings that eliminated unnecessary redundancy and improved communications between technical professionals. Recommendations resulted in reorganizing R&D functions that saved the company $450,000 in annual overhead costs.

Accomplishment statements set you apart from so many other resumes that primarily restate formal duties and responsibilities assigned to positions as "Experience." Keep focused on employers' needs by stressing your accomplishments in each of your experience statements and descriptions.

16. **INCORPORATE ACTION VERBS AND USE THE ACTIVE VOICE WHEN DESCRIBING YOUR EXPERIENCE:** The most powerful language you can use in a resume incorporates action or transitive verbs. It emphasizes taking action or initiative that goes beyond just formal assigned duties and responsibilities. If your grammar rules are a bit rusty, here are some examples of action or transitive verbs:

administered	investigated
analyzed	managed
assisted	negotiated
communicated	organized
conducted	planned
coordinated	proposed
created	recommended
designed	recruited
developed	reduced
directed	reorganized
established	revised
evaluated	selected
expanded	streamlined
generated	supervised

implemented	trained
increased	trimmed
initiated	wrote

When applied to the active voice, action or transitive verbs follow a particular grammatical pattern:

Subject	**Transitive Verb**	**Direct Objective**
I	increased	profits
I	initiated	studies
I	expanded	production

If written in the passive voice, these examples would appear in the "Experience" section of a resume in the following form—which is to be avoided:

"Profits were increased by 32 percent."

"The studies resulted in new legislation."

"Production was expanded by 24 percent."

The passive voice implies the object was subjected to some type of action but the source of the action is unknown. If written in the active voice, these same examples would read as follows:

"Increased profits by 32 percent."

"Initiated studies that resulted in new legislation."

"Expanded production by 24 percent."

When using action verbs and the active voice, the action verb implies that you, the subject, performed the action. The active voice helps elevate you to a personal performance level that gets de-emphasized, if not lost, when using the passive voice.

17. **AVOID USING THE PERSONAL PRONOUN "I":** When using the active voice, the assumption is that you are the one performing the action. As indicated in the previous principle (#16), there is no need to insert "I" when referring to your accomplishments. The use of "I" is awkward and inappropriate on a resume. It makes your resume too self-centered when you should be making it more employer-centered.

18. **USE NUMBERS AND PERCENTAGES WHENEVER POSSIBLE TO DEMONSTRATE YOUR PERFORMANCE ON PREVIOUS JOBS:** It's always best to state action and performance in some numerical fashion. For example, take this "experience" statement:

    "Increased sales each year for five straight years."

    The same statement can be stated in more powerful numerical terms that are equally truthful:

    "Increased sales annually by 23% ($147,000) during the past five years."

    Which of these statements makes a more powerful impression on employers who are looking for evidence of performance patterns that might be transferred to their organization? To state you "increased" sales without stating by "how much" leaves a great deal to the imagination. Was it 1 percent or 100 percent? $5 or $500,000? If performance differences appear impressive, state them in numerical terms.

19. **INCLUDE QUOTES RELEVANT TO YOUR PERFORMANCE:** Avoid including personal testimonials that are self-serving or are assumed to be solicited; they may appear dishonest to readers. But do include any special professional praise you

have received from a company award or from a performance evaluation. Statements such as "Received the Employee of the Year Award for outstanding performance" or "Praised by employer for 'exceptional performance' and consistently ranked in the upper 10 percent of the workforce" can be powerful additions to your resume.

20. **ELIMINATE ANY NEGATIVE REFERENCES, INCLUDING REASONS FOR LEAVING:** Keep your language focused on describing your accomplishments in positive terms. Never refer to your previous employers in negative terms and never volunteer information on why you left an employer, regardless of the reason. If you were terminated, volunteer this information only if asked to do so. This will usually occur during the job interview—not at the initial resume and letter writing stage. If an employer wants this information, he or she will ask for it during a telephone or face-to-face interview.

Keep you language focused on describing your accomplishments in positive terms.

---

21. **DO NOT INCLUDE NAMES OF SUPERVISORS:** Your experience and work history sections should only include job titles, organizations, inclusive employment dates, responsibilities, and accomplishments. Names of individuals other than yourself are subjects of interviews—not resumes.

22. **IF YOU CHOOSE A CHRONOLOGICAL RESUME, BEGIN WITH YOUR MOST RECENT JOB AND WORK BACKWARDS IN REVERSE CHRONOLOGICAL ORDER:** In a chronological resume, your present or last job should always be described first. The next job should be the one before that one and

so on. However, it is not necessary to include or provide detailed information on all jobs you ever held. Keep in mind that hiring officials are looking for patterns of performance. The best evidence of such patterns is found by examining your most recent employment—not what you did 10, 20, or 30 years ago. Include your most recent employment during the past 10 years. If you held several part-time or short-term jobs or your employment record goes back for many years, you can summarize these jobs under a single heading. For example

> **Part-time employment, 1982-1985.**
> Held several part-time positions—waitress, word processor, lab assistant—while attending college full-time.
>
> **Government employee, 1968-1981.**
> Served in several public works positions with both state and local government. Specialist on transportation policy in metropolitan areas with management-level experience.

23. **BE CONSISTENT IN HOW YOU HANDLE EACH DESCRIPTION OR SUMMARY:** The rule here is parallel construction. Each description or summary should have a similar structure and size. Use the same type of language, verb tense, grammatical structure, and punctuation.

24. **FOR EACH JOB OR SKILL, PUT THE MOST IMPORTANT INFORMATION FIRST:** Since most hiring officials want to know what you can do for them, put that information first. If you choose a chronological resume, begin with your job title and company and then stress your accomplishments. Your inclusive dates of employment should appear last, at the end of the description, rather than at the very beginning where it will tend to be the center of attention. If you choose a functional or combination resume format, put your most important accomplishments first in relation to your objective.

25. **BE SURE TO ACCOUNT FOR MAJOR TIME GAPS:** If you use a chronological resume in which inclusive employment dates

are prominent, check to see that you do not have major time gaps between jobs. You need to account for obvious time gaps. Were you in school, the military, or unemployed? If you were unemployed for a short time, you can easily handle this time gap by using years rather than exact months of a year when including dates of employment. For example, rather than state your last three jobs began and ended on these dates,

June 1985 to July 1987

December 1987 to February 1989

July 1989 to present

State they began and ended on these dates:

1985 to 1987

1987 to 1989

1989 to present

If you specify exact months you began and left jobs, you encourage the reader to look for obvious time gaps and thus raise negative questions about your employment history. If you only use years, you can cover most short-term time gaps.

26. **IF YOU ARE AN OBVIOUS "JOB HOPPER," YOU MAY WANT TO CHOOSE A FUNCTIONAL OR COMBINATION RESUME RATHER THAN A CHRONOLOGICAL RESUME:** The job descriptions associated with a chronological resume format will accentuate employment dates and make it easy for the reader to determine a pattern of career progression from one job to another. If you do not have a clear chronological pattern, you are well advised to choose another resume format that accentuates your patterns of skills.

Other Experience

27. **INCLUDE "OTHER EXPERIENCE" IF IT FURTHER STRENGTHENS YOUR OBJECTIVE IN REFERENCE TO THE EMPLOYER'S NEEDS AND CAN ACCOUNT FOR EMPLOYMENT TIME GAPS:** Standard categories of "other experience" include

- **Military service:** Describe this experience as you would any other job—emphasize your skills and accomplishments. If none seem relevant to your resume objective and employers' needs, keep this section brief by including your rank, service, assignments, and inclusive employment dates.

- **Civic/Community/Volunteer:** You may have volunteer experience that demonstrates skills and accomplishments relevant to your objective. For example, you may be involved in organizing community groups, raising funds, or operating a special program for youth. These volunteer experiences demonstrate strong organization, leadership, and communication skills.

In each case, be sure to emphasize your accomplishments as they relate to both your objective and employers' needs.

Education and Training

28. **STATE COMPLETE INFORMATION ON YOUR FORMAL EDUCATION, INCLUDING ANY HIGHLIGHTS THAT EMPHASIZE YOUR SPECIAL ABILITIES AND MOTIVA-TION:** Begin with your most recent education and provide the following details:

- Degree or diploma
- Graduation date
- Institution
- Special highlights, recognition, or achievements (optional)

The completed section might look like this:

B.A. in Sociology, 1989:
    Ohio State University, Columbus, OH
    Highlights:
        Graduated Magna Cum Laude
        Member, Phi Beta Kappa Honor Society

<u>B.S. in Criminal Justice, 1987</u>.
Ithaca College, Ithaca, NY
- Major: Law Enforcement Administration
- Minor: Management Information Systems
  G.P.A. in concentration 3.6/4.0

If your grade point and other achievements are not exceptional, do not highlight them here. They may appear mediocre to the reader and thus your education will become a negative.

29. **RECENT GRADUATES WITH LITTLE RELEVANT WORK EXPERIENCE SHOULD EMPHASIZE THEIR EDUCATIONAL BACKGROUND MORE THAN THEIR WORK EXPERIENCE:** Follow the principle that one's most important qualifications should be presented first. For recent graduates with little relevant work experience, education tends to be their most important qualification for entering the world of work. In such cases the "Education" category should immediately follow the "Objective." Include any part-time jobs, work-study programs, internships, extracurricular activities, or volunteer work under "Experience" to demonstrate your motivation, initiative, and leadership in lieu of progressive work experience.

30. **IT'S NOT NECESSARY TO INCLUDE ALL EDUCATION DEGREES OR DIPLOMAS:** If high school is your highest level of education, include only high school. If you have a degree from both a community college and four-year college, include both under education but eliminate reference to high school. Individuals with graduate degrees should only include undergraduate and graduate degrees.

31. **INCLUDE SPECIAL TRAINING RELEVANT TO YOUR OBJECTIVE AND SKILLS:** This may include specialized training courses or programs that led to certification or enhanced your knowledge, skills, and abilities. For example,

> **Additional training, 1985 to present**
> Completed several three-day workshops on written and oral communication skills: Making Formal Presentations, Briefing Techniques, Writing Memos, Audio-Visual Techniques.

When including additional education and training, include enough descriptive information so the reader will know what skills you acquired.

Professional Affiliations

32. **INCLUDE PROFESSIONAL AFFILIATIONS RELEVANT TO YOUR OBJECTIVE AND SKILLS:** While you may belong to many groups, it is not necessary to include all of them on your resume. Select only those that appear to support your objective and skills and would be of interest to an employer. Include the name, inclusive dates of membership, offices held, projects, certifications, or licenses. Normally the name of the group would be sufficient. However, should your involvement go beyond a normal passive dues-paying membership role, briefly elaborate on your contributions. For example,

> **American Society for Training and Development:** Served as President of Tidewater Virginia Chapter, 1988-1990. Developed first corporate training resource directory for Southeast Virginia.

Special Skills

33. **IT'S OKAY TO INCLUDE ANY SPECIAL SKILLS NOT COVERED IN OTHER SECTIONS OF YOUR RESUME:** These might include an ability to communicate in foreign languages, handle specific computer software programs, operate

special equipment, or demonstrate artistic talent. Again, if you have special skills relevant to your objective and skills and which should appeal to employers, include them in a separate section labeled "Special Skills" or "Other Relevant Skills."

Awards and Special Recognition

34. **INCLUDE ANY AWARDS OR SPECIAL RECOGNITION THAT DEMONSTRATE YOUR SKILLS AND ABILITIES:** Receiving recognition for special knowledge, skills, or activities communicates positive images to employers: you are respected by your peers; you are a leader; you make contributions above and beyond what is expected as "normal." However, be selective in what you include here by relating awards or special recognition received to your objective and skills. If you are seeking a computer programming position, including an award for "First Prize in Howard County's Annual Chili Cook Off" would distract from the main thrust of your resume! But receiving the "Employee of the Year" award in your last job or "Community Achievement Award" would be impressive; both awards would get the attention of employers who would be curious to learn more about the basis for receiving such awards—a good interview question.

Interests and Activities

35. **YOU MAY WANT TO INCLUDE A PERSONAL STATEMENT ON YOUR RESUME:** Normally we would not recommend including personal information on a resume. However, there is one exception and you should include such information sparingly. In addition to keeping your resume focused on your objective and skills as well as the employer's needs, you want to make you and your resume appear unique in comparison to other candidates. You may be able to achieve this in a "Personal Statement" or "Special Interests" section. This section might include hobbies or avocations. For example, if you are seeking a position you know requires a high energy level and the employer looks favorably on stable, married, family-oriented employees,

you might include some personal information as well as interests and activities that address these issues. For example, your personal data could include the following:

PERSONAL: 35 . . . in excellent health . . . married . . . children . . . enjoy challenges . . . interested in productivity.

Alternatively, you could write a personal statement about yourself so that the reader might remember you in particular. For example,

SPECIAL INTERESTS: Love the challenge of solving problems, taking initiative, and achieving results . . . be it in developing new marketing strategies, programming a computer, climbing a mountain, white water rafting, or modifying a motorcycle.

Such statements can give hobbies and special talents and interests new meaning in relation to your resume objective. But again, be very careful about including such statements. More often than not, they can be a negative, distracting the reader from the most important information included on your resume. By all means avoid trite statements that may distract from the main thrust of your resume.

Salary History or Expectations

36. **NEVER INCLUDE SALARY INFORMATION ON YOUR RESUME:** While hiring officials are interested in your salary history and expectations, there is no good reason for including this information on your resume or even in your cover letter. Salary is something that needs to be negotiated, but only after you have had a chance to learn about the value of the position as well as communicated your value to the employer. This occurs at the end of the job interview and should be the very last thing you talk about or after receiving an offer of a position. If you include salary information on your resume or in your cover letter, you are

likely to prematurely eliminate yourself from consideration—your expectations are either too high or too low.

References

37. **NEVER INCLUDE NAMES, ADDRESSES, AND PHONE NUMBERS OF YOUR REFERENCES ON YOUR RESUME:** You may want to include a final category on your resume:

    REFERENCES: Available upon request

    However, this is an empty category and can be a waste of precious resume space. It does nothing to enhance your resume. Our recommendation is to eliminate it altogether or use it to fill out a short one-page resume. Remember, you want to control your references by providing the information upon request which usually occurs during the interview stage. If you volunteer your references on the resume, your references may be unprepared to talk about you to employers. It's best to list the names, addresses, and phone numbers of your professional references on a separate sheet of paper, but take that list with you to the job interview rather than volunteer the information on your resume. Ask your references for permission to use their names and brief them on your interests in relation to the position. Make sure they have a copy of your resume for reference.

Other Information

38. **YOU MAY WANT TO INCLUDE A FEW OTHER CATEGORIES OF INFORMATION DEPENDING ON YOUR EXPERIENCE AND RELEVANCE TO EMPLOYERS:** The following categories of information may be included:

    - Certificates
    - Accreditations
    - Licenses

- Publications
- Patents
- Foreign languages
- Government clearances

However, include them only if they strengthen your qualifications in reference to the needs of hiring officials. For example, if foreign languages are important to employers, include them on your resume. If you are in a professional field that requires certificates and licenses, include the appropriate information on your resume.

Language, Style, and Tone

39. **USE AN APPROPRIATE LANGUAGE TO EXPRESS YOUR PRODUCTIVITY AND YOUR UNDERSTANDING OF THE EMPLOYER'S NEEDS:** In addition to using action verbs and the active voice, try to use the language of the employer when describing your skills and experience. Use the "jargon" of the industry in demonstrating your understanding of the employer.

40. **USE CRISP, SUCCINCT, EXPRESSIVE, AND DIRECT LANGUAGE:** Avoid poetic, bureaucratic, vernacular, and academic terms that tend to turn off readers. For example, instead of stating your objective as

> I would like to work with a consulting firm where I can develop new programs and utilize my decision-making and system-engineering experience. I hope to improve your organization's business profits.

Re-word the objective so it reads like this:

> An increasingly responsible research and development position, where proven decision-making and system engineering abilities will be used for improving productivity.

Use the first person, but do not refer to yourself as "I" or "the author." The use of action verbs and the active voice implies you are the subject. Always use active verbs and parallel sentence structure. Avoid introductory and wind-up phrases like "My duties included . . ." or "Position description reads as follows . . ." Do not use jargon unless it is appropriate to the situation.

Appearance and Visual Techniques

41. **USE APPROPRIATE HIGHLIGHTING AND EMPHASIZING TECHNIQUES:** The most important information on a one or two-page resume needs to be highlighted since many readers will only spend a few seconds skimming your resume. The most widely used highlighting and emphasizing techniques involve CAPITALIZING, underlining, *italicizing*, and **bolding** headings, words, and phrases or using bullets (•), boxes (■), hyphens (—), or asterisks (*). However, use these techniques sparingly. Overuse of highlighting and emphasizing techniques can distract from your message.

Overuse of highlighting and emphasizing techniques can distract from your message.

42. **FOLLOW THE "LESS IS MORE" RULE WHEN DECIDING FORMAT AND TYPE STYLE:** The fear of not getting all information onto one page leads some resume writers to create a very crowded and cramped resume that is most uninviting to read. Be sure to leave ample margins—at least 1" top to bottom and left to right—and white space as well as use a standard type style (Times Roman but not Helvetica) and size (10-11 point). Remember, the first thing a reader sees is layout, white space, and type

style and size. Your resume should first of all be pleasing to the eye. Less is more when writing a one-page resume.

43. **DO NOT INCLUDE SPECIAL BORDERS, GRAPHICS, OR PHOTOS UNLESS YOU ARE APPLYING FOR A JOB IN GRAPHIC ARTS OR A RELATED FIELD:** Keep the design very basic and conservative. Special graphics effects are likely to distract from your central message. However, if you are in the graphics art or related art field, you may want to dress up your resume with graphics that demonstrate your creativity and style.

Resume Length

44. **KEEP SENTENCES AND SECTIONS SHORT AND SUC-CINCT:** Keep in mind your readers will spend little time reading your resume. The shorter and more succinct you can write each section and sentence, the more powerful will be your message. Try to limit the length of each job description paragraph to five to eight lines—no more than ten.

45. **LIMIT YOUR RESUME TO ONE OR TWO PAGES:** We agree with most resume advisors that the one to two-page resume is the most appropriate, although one-page is preferable. We prefer it because it focuses the busy reader's attention on a single field of vision. It's especially reader-friendly if designed with the use of highlighting and emphasizing techniques. The one-page resume is a definite asset considering the fact that many hiring officials must review hundreds of resumes each week. Research clearly demonstrates that retention rates decrease as one's eyes move down the page and nearly vanish on a second or third page! At first the thought of writing a one or two-page resume may pose problems for you, especially if you think your resume should be a presentation of your life history. However, many executives with 25-years of experience, who make $100,000 or more a year, manage to get all their major qualifications onto a one-page resume. If they can do it, so can you. When condensing information on yourself into a one-page format, keep in mind that your

resume is an advertisement for a job interview. You only want to include enough information to grab the attention of the reader who hopefully will contact you for a job interview. If you must present your qualifications in two pages rather than one, consider making the second page a "continuation page" that provides additional details on the qualifications outlined on the first page. Two resume examples using the continuation page are presented in Chapters Five (James C. Astor) and Six (Michele R. Folger).

PRODUCTION

Employers also want to see your best professional effort at the production stage of resume writing. This involves making the right choices on paper color, weight, and texture as well as production methods. Above all, the resume they receive must be error free or they are likely to discard it as an example of incompetence.

Proofread for both form and content.

---

46. CAREFULLY PROOFREAD AND PRODUCE TWO OR THREE DRAFTS OF YOUR RESUME BEFORE PRODUC-ING THE FINAL COPIES: Be sure to carefully proofread the resume for grammatical, spelling, and punctuation errors before producing the final camera-ready copy. Any such errors will quickly disqualify you with employers. Read and reread the draft several times to see if you can improve various elements to make it more readable and eye appealing. Read for both form and content. Have someone else also review your resume and give you feedback on its form and content. Use the evaluation forms in Chapter Four to conduct both internal and external evaluations.

47. **CHOOSE WHITE, OFF-WHITE, IVORY, OR LIGHT GREY 20 TO 50 LB. BOND PAPER WITH 100% COTTON FIBER ("RAG CONTENT"):** Your choice of paper—color, weight, and texture—do make a difference to resume readers. These things say something about your professional style. Choose a poor quality paper and inappropriate color and you communicate the wrong messages to employers. There is nothing magical about ivory or off-white paper. As more and more people use these colors, off-white and ivory colors have probably lost their effectiveness. To be different, try a light grey or basic white. Indeed, white paper gives a nice bright look to what has become essentially a dull colored process. Stay with black ink or use a dark navy ink for the light grey paper. If you are applying for a creative position, you may decide to use more daring colors to better express your creative style and personality. However, stay away form dark colored papers. Resumes should have a light bright look to them. The paper should also match your cover letter and envelope.

48. **PRODUCE YOUR RESUME ON 8½ x 11 PAPER:** This is the standard business size that you should follow. Other sizes are too unconventional and thus communicate the wrong message to readers.

49. **PRINT ONLY ON ONE SIDE OF THE PAPER:** Do not produce a two-sided resume. If your resume runs two pages, print it on two separate pages and staple them together in the upper left-hand corner.

50. **USE A GOOD QUALITY MACHINE AND AN APPROPRIATE TYPEFACE:** It's best to produce your camera-ready copy (for reproduction) on a letter quality printer, preferably a laser printer, or have it typeset. Avoid manual typewriters that produce uneven type and look very amateurish. Never produce your resume on a dot matrix printer. Most such printers produce poor quality type that communicates a "mass production" quality. If you use a desktop publishing program, choose sans sarif typefaces (Times Roman, Palatino, New Century). Avoid serif typefaces

(Gothic, Helvetica, Avant Garde) which are difficult to read. Make sure you use a good quality ribbon that produces dark crisp type.

Most individuals reproduce their resume on a copy machine. Indeed, given the high quality reproduction achieved on many copy machines available at local print shops, it's not necessary to go to the expense of having your resume professionally printed. However, if you need 2000 or more copies—which is most unlikely unless you resort to a broadcast or "shot-gun" marketing approach—it may be more cost effective to have them printed. Just take your camera-ready copy, along with your choice of paper, to a local printer and have them make as many copies as you need. The cost per copy will run anywhere from 3¢ to 15¢, depending on the number of copies run. The larger the run, the cheaper will be your per unit cost.

MARKETING AND DISTRIBUTION

Your resume is only as good as your marketing and distribution plan. What, for example, will you do with your resume once you've completed it? How can you best get it into the hands of individuals who can make a difference in your job search? Are you planning to send it in response to vacancy announcements and want ads? Maybe you plan to broadcast it to hundreds of employers in the hope someone will call you for an interview? Perhaps you only want to send it to a few people who can help you with your job search? Or maybe you really don't have a plan beyond getting it produced in a "correct" form.

51. **IT'S BEST TO TARGET YOUR RESUME ON SPECIFIC EMPLOYERS RATHER THAN BROADCAST IT TO HUNDREDS OF NAMES AND ADDRESSES:** Broadcasting or "shotgunning" your resume to hundreds of potential employers will give you a false sense of making progress with your job search since you think you are actually making contact with numerous employers. However, you will be disappointed with the results. For every 100 resumes you mail, you will be lucky to get one positive response which leads to a job interview. Indeed,

many individuals report no responses after mass mailing hundreds of resumes. It's always best to **target** your resume on specific employers through one or two methods:

- **Respond to vacancy announcements or want ads:** Resumes sent in response to job listings also will give you a sense of making progress with your job search. Since competition is likely to be high for advertised positions, your chances of getting a job interview may not be good, although much better than if you broadcasted your resume to hundreds of employers who may not have openings.

- **Target employers with information on your qualifications:** The most effective way of getting job interviews is to network for information, advice, and referrals. You do this by contacting friends, professional associates, acquaintances, and others who might have information on jobs related to your interests and skills. You, in effect, attempt to uncover job vacancies before they become publicized or meet an employment need not yet recognized by employers who may create a position for you in line with your qualifications. The resume plays an important role in this networking process. In some cases, you will be referred to someone who is interested in seeing your resume; when that happens, send it along with a cover letter and follow-up your mailing with a telephone call. In other cases, you will conduct informational interviews with individuals who can give you advice and referrals relevant to your career interests. You should take your resume to the informational interview and at the very end of your meeting ask your informant to critique your resume. In the process of examining your resume, your informant is likely to give you good feedback for further revising your resume as well as refer you and your resume to others. If you regularly repeat this networking and informational interviewing process, within a few weeks you should begin landing job interviews directly related to the qualifications you outlined in your dynamite resume!

52. **YOUR RESUME SHOULD ALWAYS BE ACCOMPANIED BY A COVER LETTER:** A resume unaccompanied by a cover letter is a naked resume—like going to a job interview barefoot. The cover letter is very important in relation to the resume. After all, if sent through the mail, the letter is the first thing a hiring official reads before getting to the resume. If the letter is interesting enough, the person proceeds to read the resume. A well-crafted cover letter should complement rather than repeat the content of your resume. It should grab the reader's attention, communicate your purpose, and convince the reader to take action. See our *Dynamite Cover Letters* book for an extended discussion of the principles of effective cover letter writing, production, distribution, and follow-up. Neglect the importance of the cover letter and you may effectively kill your resume!

Neglect the importance of the cover letter and you may effectively kill your resume!

---

53. **NEVER ENCLOSE LETTERS OF RECOMMENDATION, TRANSCRIPTS, OR OTHER INFORMATION WITH YOUR RESUME UNLESS REQUESTED TO DO SO:** Unsolicited letters of recommendation are negatives. Readers know they have been specially produced to impress them and thus they may question your integrity. Unsolicited transcripts also may communicate negative messages unless you have perfect grades. Such information merely distracts from your resume and cover letter. It does not contribute to getting a job interview. It indicates you do

not know what you are doing by including such information with your resume and letter.

54. **YOUR RESUME SHOULD BE ADDRESSED TO A SPECIFIC PERSON:** Always try to get the correct name and position of the person who should receive your resume. Unless you are specifically instructed to do so, addressing your correspondence to "Dear Sir," "Director of Personnel," or "To Whom It May Concern" is likely to result in lost correspondence; the mail room may treat it as junk mail. If you later follow-up your correspondence with a phone call, you have no one to communicate with. A couple of phone calls to the organization should quickly result in the proper name. Just call the switchboard or a receptionist and ask the following:

> *"I need to send some correspondence to the person in charge of _____. Whom might that be? And what is the correct address?"*

Keep in mind that the people who have the power to hire are usually not in the Personnel Office; they tend to be the heads of operating units. So target your resume accordingly!

People who have the power to hire are usually not in the Personnel Office.

---

55. **ENCLOSE YOUR RESUME AND LETTER IN A MATCHING NO. 10 BUSINESS ENVELOPE OR IN A 9 x 12 ENVELOPE:** We prefer the 9 x 12 envelope because it keeps your correspondence flat and has greater presence than the No. 10 business envelope. Keep all your stationery matching, including

the 9 x 12 envelope. If, however, it's difficult to find a matching 9 x 12 envelope, go with a white or buff-colored envelope or use a U.S. Postal Service "Priority Mail" envelope.

56. **TYPE THE ENVELOPE OR MAILING LABEL RATHER THAN HAND-WRITE THE ADDRESS:** Hand-written addresses look too personal and amateurish. They do not gain more attention nor generate more positive responses. Typed addresses look more professional.

57. **SEND YOUR CORRESPONDENCE BY FIRST-CLASS OR PRIORITY MAIL OR SPECIAL NEXT-DAY SERVICES, AND USE STAMPS:** If you want to get the recipient's immediate attention, send your correspondence in one of those colorful next-day air service envelopes provided by the U.S. Postal Service, Federal Express, UPS, or other carriers or couriers. However, first-class or priority mail will usually get your correspondence delivered within two to three days. It's best to affix a nice commemorative stamp rather than use a postage meter. A stamp helps personalize your mailing piece.

58. **NEVER FAX YOUR RESUME UNLESS ASKED TO DO SO BY YOUR RECIPIENT:** It is presumptuous for anyone to fax their resume to an employer without express permission to do so. Such faxes are treated as junk mail and are viewed as an unwarranted invasion of privacy. If asked to fax your correspondence, be sure to follow it up by mailing a copy of the original and indicating you sent materials by fax on a specific date as requested. The poor quality transmission of most fax machines will not do justice to the overall quality of your resume.

FOLLOW-UP

Follow-up remains the least understood but most important step in any job search. Whatever you do, make sure you follow-up **all** of your job search activities. If you fail to follow-up, you are likely to get little or no response to your job search initiatives. Follow-up means taking action that gets results.

59. **FOLLOW-UP YOUR RESUME WITHIN SEVEN DAYS OF MAILING IT:** Do not let too much time lapse between when you mailed your resume and when you contact the resume recipient. Seven days should give the recipient sufficient time to examine your communication and decide on your future status. If not, your follow-up will assist in making a decision.

60. **THE BEST FOLLOW-UP FOR A MAILED RESUME IS A TELEPHONE CALL:** Don't expect your resume recipient to take the initiative in calling you for an interview. State in your cover letter that you will call the recipient at a particular time to discuss your resume:

> I will call your office on the morning of March 17 to see if a meeting can be scheduled at a convenient time.

And be sure you indeed follow-up with a phone call at the designated time. If you have difficulty contacting the individual, try three times to get through. After the third try, leave a message as well as write a letter as an alternative to the telephone follow-up. In this letter, inquire about the status of your resume and thank the individual for his or her consideration.

61. **FOLLOW-UP YOUR FOLLOW-UP WITH A NICE THANK-YOU LETTER:** Regardless of the outcome of your follow-up phone call, send a nice thank-you letter based upon your conversation. You thank the letter recipient for taking the time to speak with you and to reiterate your interest in the position.

The examples found in the remainder of this book are based upon many of these resume writing and production principles. Examine those examples for ideas on how to develop each resume section. But be sure **you write your own resume** based upon the above principles rather than on the subsequent examples.

Chapter Four

EVALUATE YOUR RESUME COMPETENCE

Once you complete your resume, be sure to evaluate it according to the principles in Chapter Three. You should conduct two evaluations: internal and external. An internal evaluation involves you examining the resume in reference to self-evaluation criteria. An external evaluation involves having someone else critique your resume for its overall effectiveness.

INTERNAL EVALUATION

Examine your resume in reference to the following evaluation criteria. Respond to each statement by circling the appropriate number to the right that most accurately describes your resume:

> 1 = Strong Agree
> 2 = Agree
> 3 = So-So
> 4 = Disagree
> 5 = Strongly Disagree

The numbers at the end of each statement correspond to each principle previously outlined in Chapter Three. Refer to these principles for further clarification.

WRITING

1. Wrote the resume myself—no creative plagiarizing from others' resume examples. (#1)   1   2   3   4   5

2. Conducted a thorough self-assessment which became the basis for writing each resume section. (#1)   1   2   3   4   5

3. Have a plan of action that relates my resume to other job search activities. (#2)   1   2   3   4   5

4. Selected an appropriate resume format that best presents my interests, skills, and experience. (#3)   1   2   3   4   5

5. Included all essential information categories in the proper order. (#4-5)   1   2   3   4   5

6. Eliminated all extraneous information unrelated to my objective and employers' needs (date, picture, race, religion, political affiliation, age, sex, height, weight, marital status, health, hobbies) or better saved for discussion in the interview—salary history and references. (#6)   1   2   3   4   5

7. Put the most important information first. (#5)   1   2   3   4   5

8. Resume is oriented to the future rather than to the past. (#4)   1   2   3   4   5

9. Contact information is complete—name,
   address, and phone number. No P.O. Box
   numbers or nicknames. (#7-8)   1   2   3   4   5

10. Limited abbreviations to a few
    accepted words. (#8)   1   2   3   4   5

11. Contact information attractively
    formatted to introduce the resume. (#8)   1   2   3   4   5

12. Included a thoughtful employer-oriented
    objective that incorporates both skills
    and benefits. (#9)   1   2   3   4   5

13. Objective clearly communicates to
    employers what I want to do, can do,
    and will do for them. (#9)   1   2   3   4   5

14. Objective is neither too general
    nor too specific. (#10)   1   2   3   4   5

15. Objective serves as the central
    organizing element for all other
    sections of the resume. (#11)   1   2   3   4   5

16. Considered including a "Summary
    of Qualification" section. (#12)   1   2   3   4   5

17. Elaborated work experience in detail,
    emphasizing my skills, abilities,
    and achievements. (#13 & #15)   1   2   3   4   5

18. Each "Experience" section is short
    and to the point. (#14)   1   2   3   4   5

19. Consistently used action verbs and
    the active voice. (#16)   1   2   3   4   5

20. Did not refer to myself as "I". (#17)   1   2   3   4   5

21. Used specifics—numbers and percentages—
to highlight my performance. (#18)   1   2   3   4   5

22. Included quotations about my
performance from previous
employers. (#19)   1   2   3   4   5

23. Eliminated any negative references,
including reasons for leaving. (#20)   1   2   3   4   5

24. Does not include names of
supervisors. (#21)   1   2   3   4   5

25. Summarized my most recent job and
then included other jobs in reverse
chronological order. (#22)   1   2   3   4   5

26. Descriptions of "Experience" are
consistent. (#23)   1   2   3   4   5

27. Put the most important information
on my skills first when summarizing
my "Experience." (#24)   1   2   3   4   5

28. No time gaps nor "job hopping"
apparent to reader. (#25-26)   1   2   3   4   5

29. Documented "other experience" that
might strengthen my objective and
decided to either include or exclude
it on the resume. (#27)   1   2   3   4   5

30. Included complete information on
my educational background, including
important highlights. (#28)   1   2   3   4   5

31. If a recent graduate with little
relevant work experience, emphasized
educational background more than
work experience. (#29)   1   2   3   4   5

32. Put education in reverse chronological order and eliminated high school if a college graduate. (#30)   1 2 3 4 5

33. Included special education and training relevant to my major interests and skills. (#31)   1 2 3 4 5

34. Included professional affiliations and membership relevant to my objective and skills; highlighted any major contributions. (#32)   1 2 3 4 5

35. Documented any special skills not included elsewhere on resume and included those that appear relevant to employers' needs. (#33)   1 2 3 4 5

36. Included awards or special recognition that further documents my skills and achievements. (#34)   1 2 3 4 5

37. Weighed pros and cons of including a personal statement on my resume. (#35)   1 2 3 4 5

38. Did not mention salary history or expectations. (#36)   1 2 3 4 5

39. Did not include names, addresses, and phone number of references. (#37)   1 2 3 4 5

40. Included additional information to enhance the interest of employers. (#38)   1 2 3 4 5

41. Used a language appropriate for the employer, including terms that associate me with the industry. (#39)   1 2 3 4 5

42. My language is crisp, succinct, expressive, and direct. (#40)   1 2 3 4 5

43. Used highlighting and emphasizing
    techniques to make the resume
    most readable. (#41)   1   2   3   4   5

44. Resume has an inviting, uncluttered
    look, incorporating sufficient white
    space and using a standard type
    style and size. (#42)   1   2   3   4   5

45. Kept the design very basic and
    conservative. (#43)   1   2   3   4   5

46. Kept sentences and sections
    short and succinct. (#44)   1   2   3   4   5

47. Resume runs one or two pages. (#45)   1   2   3   4   5

PRODUCTION

48. Carefully proofread and produced
    two or three drafts which were
    subjected to both internal and
    external evaluations before
    producing the final copies. (#46)   1   2   3   4   5

49. Chose a standard color and quality
    of paper. (#47)   1   2   3   4   5

50. Used 8½ x 11 paper. (#48)   1   2   3   4   5

51. Printed resume on only one
    side of paper. (#49)   1   2   3   4   5

52. Used a good quality machine and
    an easy-to-read typeface. (#50)   1   2   3   4   5

MARKETING AND DISTRIBUTION

53. Targeted resume toward specific
    employers. (#51)   1   2   3   4   5

54. Used resume properly for networking and informational interviewing activities. (#51)   1 2 3 4 5

55. Resume accompanied by a dynamite cover letter. (#52)   1 2 3 4 5

56. Only enclosed a cover letter with my resume—no other unsolicited materials included. (#53)   1 2 3 4 5

57. Addressed to a specific name and position. (#54)   1 2 3 4 5

58. Mailed resume and cover letter in a matching No. 10 business envelope or in a 9 x 12 envelope. (#55)   1 2 3 4 5

59. Typed address on envelope. (#56)   1 2 3 4 5

60. Sent correspondence by first-class or priority mail or special next-day services; affixed attractive commemorative stamps. (#57)   1 2 3 4 5

FOLLOW-UP

61. Followed-up the mailed resume within 7 days. (#59)   1 2 3 4 5

62. Used the telephone for following up. (#60)   1 2 3 4 5

63. Followed-up the follow-up with a nice thank-you letter. (#61)   1 2 3 4 5

TOTAL

Add the numbers you circled to the right of each statement to get a cumulative score. If your score is higher than 85, you need to work on improving various aspects of your resume. Go back and institute the necessary changes to create a truly dynamite resume.

EXTERNAL EVALUATION

In many respects the external resume evaluation plays the most crucial role in your overall job search. It helps you get remembered which, in turn, leads to referrals and job leads.

The best way to conduct an external evaluation is to circulate your resume to two or more individuals. Choose people whose opinions you value for being objective, frank, and thoughtful. Do not select friends and relatives who might flatter you with positive comments. Professional acquaintances or people you don't know personally but whom you admire may be good candidates for this type of evaluation.

An ideal evaluator has experience in hiring people in your area of expertise. In addition to sharing their experience with you, they may refer you to other individuals who would be interested in your qualifications. You will encounter many of these individuals in the process of networking and conducting informational interviews. You, in effect, conduct an external evaluation of your resume with this individual during the informational interview. At the very end of the informational interview you should ask the person to examine your resume; you want to elicit comments on how you can better strengthen the resume. Ask him or her the following questions:

> *"If you don't mind, would you look over my resume? Perhaps you could comment on its clarity or make suggestions for improving it?"*

> *"How would you react to this resume if you received it from a candidate? Does it grab your attention and interest you enough to talk with me?"*

> *"If you were writing this resume, what changes would you make? Any additions, deletions, or modifications?"*

Answers to these questions should give you invaluable feedback for improving both the form and content of your resume. You will be eliciting advice from people whose opinions count. However, it is not necessary to incorporate all such advice. Some evaluators, while well-meaning, will not provide you with sound advice. Instead, they may reinforce many of the pitfalls found in weak resumes.

Another way to conduct an external evaluation is to develop a checklist of evaluation criteria and give it, along with your resume, to individuals whose opinions and expertise you value. Unlike the evaluation criteria used for the internal evaluation, the evaluation criteria for the external evaluation should be more general. Have your evaluator examine your resume in relation to these instructions and criteria:

Circle the number that best characterizes various aspects of my resume as well as include any recommendations on how to best improve the resume:

    1 = Excellent
    2 = Okay
    3 = Weak

Recommendations for
improvement

1. Overall appearance   1   2   3   _____

2. Layout   1   2   3   _____

3. Clarity   1   2   3   _____

4. Consistency   1   2   3   _____

5. Readability   1   2   3   _____

6. Language   1   2   3   _____

7. Organization   1   2   3   _____

8. Content/completeness   1   2   3   _____

9. Length   1   2   3   _____

10. Contact information/header 1   2   3   _____

11. Objective   1   2   3   _____

12. Experience   1   2   3   _____

13. Skills   1   2   3   _____

14. Achievements   1   2   3   _____

15. Education   1   2   3   _____

16. Other information   1   2   3   _____

17. Paper color   1   2   3   _____

18. Paper size and stock   1   2   3   _____

19. Overall production quality 1   2   3   _____

20. Potential effectiveness   1   2   3   _____

SUMMARY EVALUATION: _____

_____

_____

_____

_____

After completing these external evaluations and incorporating useful suggestions for further improving the quality of your resume, it's a good idea to send a copy of your revised resume to those individuals who were helpful in giving you advice. Thank them for their time and thoughtful comments. Ask them to keep you in mind should they hear of anyone who might be interested in your experience and skills. In so doing, you will be demonstrating your appreciation and thoughtfulness as well as reminding them to remember you for further information, advice, and referrals.

In the end, **being remembered in reference to your resume** is one of the most important goals you want to repeatedly achieve during your job search. As you will quickly discover, your most effective job search strategy involves networking with your resume. You want to share information, by way of the informational interview, about your interests and qualifications with those who can give advice, know about job vacancies, or can refer you to individuals who have the power to hire. Your resume, and especially this external evaluation, plays a critical role in furthering this process.

Chapter Five

RESUME TRANSFORMATIONS

Most resumes can be improved by following several rules outlined in Chapter Three. If you already have a completed resume, you should review it in reference to the evaluation criteria outlined in Chapter Four.

Better still, let's look at four sets of examples that incorporate many of our principles of effective resume writing. These are actual examples from individuals who started with weak resume writing skills and with a little help managed to transform an ordinary resume into a dynamite resume that led to interviews and job offers.

FROM ORDINARY TO DYNAMITE RESUMES

Transforming an ordinary resume into a dynamite resume is not difficult if you keep focused on your purpose and incorporate a few basic principles of effective resume writing. Indeed, after more than 12 years of resume writing, the single most important problem we have encountered with clients has been their inability to keep their writing, as well as their job search, **focused** around clear goals and purposes. The most important guiding principle is that your resume should be **employer-centered** rather than self-centered. It should respond to the **needs of employers** rather than merely catalog your work history and express some interests. Everything you decide to put in your resume, including every sentence and phrase you craft, must be done in reference to this principle. Keep everything focused around your purpose. You must separate those things that belong in a resume from those things that are best discussed in a job interview, such as salary, references, reasons for leaving previous jobs, names of supervisors, employment gaps. The resume should be designed to generate positive responses about you as both a professional and person rather than raise and/or answer questions in a negative manner.

Always keep your resume simple and focused on its purpose.

Always keep your resume simple and focused on its purpose—**to elicit action on the part of the reader**. Like good advertising copy, you want to provide just enough interesting information to motivate your reader to take action. If you fail to keep this purpose in mind, you are likely to produce anything but a dynamite resume.

If written properly, your resume will begin taking on a life of its own. It will capsulize in one page what exactly you

- **Want to do:** a statement of your goals and objectives.

- **Can do:** statements of your actual performance.

- **Will do in the future:** a probability conclusion drawn by the reader based upon a summary analysis of your resume content.

It should clearly address the needs of employers. It should answer these important questions:

- What can this person do for me?

- How will this person fit into our organization?

- Will this person be able to solve our problems and grow within our organization?

- Should I contact this person for an interview to answer several other equally important questions?

The following resume transformations speak to these principles. They focus on the needs of employers in attempting to motivate them to take action.

GAIL TOPPER

The first case, Gail Topper (page 88), is an actual case study. While it is not a typical case, it does emphasize how to handle important employment problems with different types of resumes. The individual had held several full-time positions as typist, secretary, receptionist, and sales clerk while working her way through college. After graduation, she continued in her former occupation. Wanting to break out of the "once a secretary, always a secretary" pattern, she has several resume options for changing careers. Everything appearing in these resumes is true. One of the major differences is the truth is better communicated to her advantage in some resumes than in others.

The first resume represents the **traditional chronological or "obituary" resume**. It stresses skills and accomplishments in relationship to an objective. In this resume, Gail presents jobs that don't strengthen her objective.

The **improved chronological resume** on page 93 presents a totally different picture of Gail Topper. It stresses skills and accomplishments in relationship to an objective. In this resume Gail Topper presents those jobs which strengthen her objective.

The **functional resume** on page 94 presents another picture of this individual's qualifications. Here, employment dates and job titles are eliminated in favor of presenting transferable skills and accomplishments. While this resume is ideal for someone entering the job market with little job related experience, this resume does not take advantage of this individual's work experience with specific employers.

The **combination resume** on page 95 is ideal for this particular person. It minimizes employment dates and job titles, stresses transferable skills and accomplishments, and includes work history. The individual appears purposeful, skilled, and experienced.

The resume letter on page 96 also is a good alternative for this person. It is designed to open doors without the traditional resume. The individual can present one of the resumes—preferably the combination resume—to the employer at some later date.

Notice the secretarial experience does not appear on the improved chronological, functional, or combination resumes. If it did, it would tend to stereotype this individual prior to being invited to an interview. It is important, however, that this individual be able to explain the secretarial experience during the interview, especially how it will make her a particularly good salesperson—knows the particular equipment and problems from the perspective of those who will use it on a day-to-day basis.

This individual was pleased with her resume—she thought it outlined a great deal of education and work experience that would appeal to potential employers. However, if you examine this resume carefully, you will notice this individual violated several principles of good resume writing. First, she includes a great deal of **extraneous information**, beginning with weight, height, age, health, and marital status in the header to including irrelevant hobbies as well as names and addresses of references. None of this information relates to any bonefide hiring criteria. It distracts from the resume as well as raises possible negative questions.

This resume also clearly **lacks a focus**. Worst of all, it **raises many negative questions and conclusions** about the individual's goals, interests, and employment history. Remember, employers look for **patterns of work behavior** that will provide clues about the individual's **probable future performance**. Three unflattering patterns are apparent from this resume:

- She appears to be a job hopper.

- She's someone with an unfocused career.

TRADITIONAL CHRONOLOGICAL RESUME

RESUME

Gail S. Topper	Weight:	122 lbs.
136 W. Davis St.	Height:	5'4"
Washington, DC 20030	Born:	8/4/54
202-465-9821	Health:	Good
	Marital Status:	Married

Education

1980-1983   George Mason University, Fairfax, Virginia. I
             received my B.A. in Comunications.

1977-1979   Northern Virginia Community College, Annandale,
             Virginia. I completed my A.A. degree.

1972-1976   Harrisonburg High School, Harrisonburg, Virginia.

Work Experience

2/14/86 to present: Secretary, MCT Coporation, 2381 Rhode
                     Island Ave., Philadelphia, Pennsylvania 19322.

2/30/84 to 2/9/86: Secretary, Martin Computer Services, 391 Old
                    Main Rd., Charleston, South Carolina 37891.

4/21/83 to 2/20/84: Secretary, STR Systems, Inc., 442 Virginia
                     Ave., Rm. 21, Washington, D.C. 20011.

9/28/82 to 1/4/83: Typist, NTC Corporation, 992 Fairy Avenue,
                    Springfield, Virginia 22451.

1/9/82 to 7/30/92: Secretary, Foreign Language Department,
                    George Mason University, Fairfax, Virginia 22819

3/1/80 to 9/14/81: Salesclerk, Sears Reobuck & Co., 294
                    Wisconsin Avenue, Boston, Massachusetts 08233

5/3/77 to 2/1/79: Salesclerk, JT's, 332 Monroe St., New Orleans,
                   Louisiana 70014.

1972-1976: Held several jobs as cook, counter help, salesclerk,
            typist, and secretarial assistant.

Community Involvement

1987 to prsent: Sunday school teacher. Grace Methodist Church.
Falls Church, Virginia.

1983: Volunteer. Red Cross. Falls Church, Virginia.

1979: Stage crew member. Community Theatre Group.
New Orleans, Louisiana

1978: Extra. Community Theatre Group. Annandale, Virginia.

Hobbies

I like to swim, cook, garden, bicycle, and listen to rock music.

Personal Statement

I have good mannual dexterity developed by working back stage in theatrical productions and working with various office machines. I can operate IBM Mag Card A and II typeriters, dictaphones, IBM 6640 (ink jet printer), various duplicating machines, and several copying machines. Familiar with addressograph. I am willing to relocate nad travel.

References

John R. Teems, Manager, Martin Computer Services, 391 Old Dominion Rd., Annandale, Virginia 20789

James Stevens, Secretary, STR Systems, Inc., 442 Virginia Ave., Rm. 21, Washington, D.C. 20011.

Alice Bears, Assistant Personnel Director, MCT Corporation, 2381 Rhode Island Ave., Philadelphia, Pennsylvania 19322

Also contact the Office of Career Planning and Placement at George Mason University.

- She's an educated secretary/typist with a communication major who makes spelling mistakes!

Based on previous experience, the employer also might conclude this is possibly someone with low self-esteem.

An employer reading this resume is likely to raise these negative questions and draw several negative conclusions:

- What is it she wants to do?

- What skills does she have?

- Why has she changed jobs so often?

- I think this person will quit her next job within one year.

- Maybe she's a secretary, but she could be a salesclerk, a typist, or a computer operator.

- Can't spell!

- I think she'll leave her next job within a few months—I won't give her more than a year or two, maximum.

- I won't waste my time on this one!

You should never have such questions raised nor conclusions drawn about your resume. This is truly an obituary resume, destined to join the graveyard of so many other ineffective resumes.

This resume has numerous problems, but the most serious problem is found in the **choice of resume format**. Remember, resume format helps structure one's thinking about an individual's qualifications. Moreover, you always want to put your most important information first. If you present dates first, you invite the reader to analyze your resume chronologically and thus ask chronological questions. The reader will begin looking for time gaps as well as average length of employment with each employer.

Gail Topper obviously has a checkered employment history when she presents her experience in chronological terms. Unfortunately, employment dates were her weakest point but she presented them initially and thus did just the opposite of what she should have done—presented her weakest points first! In fact, the reason for making so many job changes was her family situation—her husband was in the U.S. Navy and was transferred often—something employers would not know except in a job interview after asking *"Why did you leave your job at companies A, B, C, D, and E?"* Since she will never get to the interview stage with most employers, she let the reader raise a negative question then intuitively answer it:

> *"Why did she change jobs so often. She's probably an unstable employee who may lack good work habits. We don't need to hire this problem!"*

The reality is that she took sales, typing, and secretarial jobs because she was unable to build a career in such a mobile family situation. These jobs actually accentuated her weaknesses—regardless of all her education and training, she couldn't spell! She was dyslexic. She had excellent skills, many unrelated to secretarial work, and was an outstanding worker. But Uncle Sam called her husband to often pack up and move to another military installation. When looking for new employment, she managed to always shoot herself in the foot with this type of resume. Her biggest problem was in putting all her experience into a traditional chronological format which further accentuated her unstable work history and communicated low value to potential employers.

There were other ways she could have presented her qualifications to employers, but she didn't know how to do it. In fact, she thought she already had a good resume—she had used other examples as the basis for writing her own resume rather than generate important job and career information on herself. The first thing she needed to do was to undergo a complete self-assessment for identifying her major interests, skills, and abilities. She needed this information in order to focus her resume around an objective and to develop an appropriate language—using action verbs and the active voice—for writing each resume section. Since her employment dates were her weakest points, she had to abandon the traditional chronological resume in favor of other resume formats that could best present her strongest qualifications first.

The process of transforming this resume in reality also became a process of self-discovery. It was a personal journey into the world of career planning which involves such issues as self-esteem, identifying interests and values, charting goals, specifying achievements, and planning for the next 10 years of her worklife. She went through both a personal and professional transformation; she learned a great deal about herself—her goals, interests, skills, and abilities which were previously buried under the irrelevant baggage of the traditional chronological resume. Above all, she discovered she was pursuing her career weaknesses (remember, she can't spell) rather than her strengths which she had yet to systematically identify. In other words, she was in the all the wrong jobs.

In the process of creating a new resume, she literally transformed her whole job and career orientation. Indeed, the resume writing exercise became an important transformation in her life. The good news is that she has found terrific jobs ever since! Her husband, who has since retired from the U.S. Navy, has also applied the same principles in writing his own dynamite resume which has resulted in similar career success.

After much soul searching centered on identifying her major strengths—motivated abilities and skills (MAS)—we were able to point her in more fruitful career directions that emphasized what was **right** about her. She developed a new resume with a new career objective which was supported by patterns of skills and accomplishments. Moving away from the traditional chronological resume, which was inappropriate given her background and career interests, we developed four different types of resumes using other resume formats: Improved Chronological, Functional, Combination, and Resume Letter. Examine each of these examples carefully on pages 93-96. Keep in mind that everything in these resumes is true, but we've been able to refocus this person's life around clear goals, patterns of accomplishments, and the needs of employers. You will quickly see that this person has many **strengths** that were not apparent from reading her Traditional Chronological Resume.

IMPROVED CHRONOLOGICAL RESUME

GAIL S. TOPPER
136 West Davis Street
Washington, DC 20030   202/465-9821

OBJECTIVE: A professional sales position. . . leading to management. . . in information processing where administrative and technical experience, initiative, and interpersonal skills will be used for maximizing sales and promoting good customer relations.

EDUCATION: **B.A. in Communication, 1983**
George Mason University, Fairfax, Virginia.
- Courses in interpersonal communication, psychology, and public speaking.
- Worked full-time in earning 100% of educational and personal expenses.

TECHNICAL EXPERIENCE: **MCT Corporation, 2381 Rhode Island Avenue, Philadelphia, PA 20033:** Office management and materials production responsibilities. Planned and re-organized word processing center. Initiated time and cost studies, which saved company $30,000 in additional labor costs. Improved efficiency of personnel. 1986 to present.

Martin Computer Services, 391 Main Rd., Charleston, SC 37891: Communication and materials production responsibilities. Handled customer complaints. Created new tracking and filing system for Mag cards. Improved turnaround time for documents production. Operated Savin word processor. 1984 to 1986.

STR Systems, 442 Virginia Avenue, Rm. 21, Washington, DC 20011: Equipment operation and production responsibilities. Operated Mag card and high speed printers: IBM 6240, Mag A,I,II,IBM 6640. Developed and organized technical reference room for more effective use of equipment. 1983-1984.

SALES EXPERIENCE: **Sears Roebuck & Co., 294 Wisconsin Avenue, Boston, MA 08233:** Promoted improved community relations with company. Solved customer complaints. Reorganized product displays. Handled orders. 1980 to 1982.

JT's, 332 Monroe St., New Orleans, LA 70014: Recruited new clients. Maintained inventory. Developed direct sales approach. 1977 to 1979.

FUNCTIONAL RESUME

GAIL S. TOPPER

136 West Davis St.   Washington, DC 20030   202/465-9821

OBJECTIVE: A professional sales position. . .leading to management. . .
in information processing where administrative and
technical experience, initiative, and interpersonal skills will
be used for maximizing sales and promoting good
customer relations.

EDUCATION: **B.A. in Communication, 1983**
George Mason University, Fairfax, Virginia.
- Courses in interpersonal communication,
  psychology, and public speaking.
- Worked full-time in earning 100% of educational
  and personal expenses.

AREAS OF EFFECTIVENESS

SALES/   Promoted improved community relations with business.
CUSTOMER   Solved customer complaints. Recruited new clients.
RELATIONS: Re-organized product displays. Maintained inventory.
                    Received and filled orders.

PLANNING/   Planned and re-organized word processing center.
ORGANIZING: Initiated time and cost studies, which saved company
                    additional labor costs and improved efficiency of
                    personnel. Developed and organized technical reference
                    room for more effective utilization of equipment. Created
                    new tracking and filing system for Mag cards which
                    resulted in eliminating redundancy and improving
                    turnaround time.

TECHNICAL: Eight years of experience in operating Mag card and high
                    speed printers: IBM 6240, Mag A, I,II,IBM 6640, and
                    Savin word processor.

PERSONAL: 30. . .excellent health. . .enjoy challenges. . .interested in
                    productivity. . .willing to relocate and travel.

REFERENCES: Available upon request.

COMBINATION RESUME

GAIL S. TOPPER

136 West Davis St.	Washington, DC 20030	202/465-9821

OBJECTIVE: A professional sales position. . .leading to management. . . in information processing where administrative and technical experience, initiative, and interpersonal skills will be used for maximizing sales and promoting good customer relations.

AREAS OF EFFECTIVENESS

SALES/ CUSTOMER RELATIONS: Promoted improved community relations with business. Solved customer complaints. Recruited new clients. Re-organized product displays. Maintained inventory. Received and filled orders.

PLANNING/ ORGANIZING Planned and re-organized word processing center. Initiated time and cost studies, which saved company additional labor costs and improved efficiency of personnel. Developed and organized technical reference room for more effective utilization of equipment. Created new tracking and filing system for Mag cards which resulted in eliminating redundancy and improving turnaround time.

TECHNICAL: Eight years of experience in operating Mag card and high speed printers: IBM 6240, Mag A,I,II,IBM 6640, and Savin word processor.

EMPLOYMENT EXPERIENCE: MCT Corporation, Philadelphia, PA
Martin Computer Services, Charleston, SC
STR Systems, Inc., Washington, DC
NTC Corporation, Springfield, VA

EDUCATION: <u>**B.A. in Communication, 1983**</u>
George Mason University, Fairfax, Virginia.
- Courses in interpersonal communication, psychology, and public speaking.
- Worked full-time in earning 100% of educational and personal expenses.

PERSONAL: 30. . .excellent health. . .enjoy challenges. . .interested in productivity. . .willing to relocate and travel.

RESUME LETTER

136 W. Davis St.
Washington, DC 20030
January 7, 199___

James C. Thomas, President
Advanced Technology Corporation
721 West Stevens Road
Bethesda, MD 20110

Dear Mr. Thomas:

Advanced Technology's word processing equipment is the finest on the market today. I know because I have used different systems over the past eight years. Your company is the type of organization I would like to be associated with.

Over the next few months I will be seeking a sales position with an information processing company. My technical, sales, and administrative experience include:

- Technical: eight years operating Mag card and high speed printers: IBM 6240, MAG A,I,II,IBM 6640, and Savin word processor.

- Sales: recruited clients; maintained inventory; received and filled orders; improved business-community relations.

- Administrative: planned and re-organized word processing center; created new tracking and filing systems; initiated time and cost studies which reduced labor costs by $30,000 and improved efficiency of operations.

In addition, I have a bachelor's degree in communication with emphasis on public speaking, interpersonal communication, and psychology.

Your company interests me very much. I would appreciate an opportunity to meet with you to discuss how my qualifications can best meet your needs. I will call your office next Monday, January 18, to arrange a meeting with you at a convenient time.

Thank you for your consideration.

Sincerely yours,

Gail S. Topper

KAREN JONES

The second set of examples (pages 98-103) relates to a situation faced by thousands of educators each year—making a career transition from education to some other occupational field. These resumes also are relevant to millions of other individuals who decide to make career changes at some point in their worklifes. The question facing them is how to best present their past work history which is not directly related to jobs held in another career field. How can you appear qualified when you don't have direct work experience in the other field? The secret is to focus on **transferable skills**—those skills which are common in many different occupational fields—and then present them in an appropriate resume format that will stress the particular talents of the career changer. We apply this strategy in this set of examples.

In these examples, our subject, Karen Jones, begins with the Traditional Chronological Resume and transforms it into an Improved Chronological, Functional, and Combination resume as well as a Resume Letter. Each resume format tends to emphasize different aspects of her qualifications. For example, the Traditional Chronological Resume on pages 98-99 basically tells prospective employers that she is a teacher without career goals. It lacks an objective, includes extraneous information, and lists work history by dates. Accentuating her negatives, this is an inappropriate resume for such a career changer.

The Improved Chronological Resume on page 100 gives us a clearer picture of what she wants to do as well as what she has done in the past. However, it still emphasizes the fact that she is a former teacher. This format does not enable her to emphasize those skills that are most relevant to her objective. Nonetheless, this is a great improvement over her Traditional Chronological Resume.

The Functional, Combination, and Letter resumes on pages 101-103 enable Karen Jones to better demonstrate her transferable skills in relation to a desired non-teaching position. Any of these resume formats would be most appropriate for someone making a significant career change.

TRADITIONAL CHRONOLOGICAL RESUME

Karen Jones

Address: 1234 Main Street
                 Norfolk, VA 23508

Telephone: Area Code 804, Number 440-4321

Marital Status: Divorced; 2 children; ages 10 and 12
Date of Birth: April 1, 1952
Health: Excellent
Height: 5 feet, 4 inches
Weight: 125 lbs.

Educational Background:

University of Virginia, Charlottesville, Virginia. Bachelor of Arts Degree in English Literature with Certification in Secondary Education, June 1974.

Old Dominion University, Norfolk, Virginia. Master of Science Degree in Secondary Education, June 1979.

Work History:

1980 to Present—Norfolk Public Schools, Norfolk, VA.
English Teacher—I teach 11th and 12th grade English composition and creative writing classes. I have also served as co-director of the senior class play, coordinated student fund raising activities, and chaired the school committee which developed recruiting and public relations materials. I have given speeches at student events and helped write speeches for the school administration.

1975-1980—Full-time Homemaker.

1973-1975—Chesapeake Public Schools, Chesapeake, Virginia.
English Teacher—I taught 10th and 11th grade composition classes.

Community Involvements:

Toastmaster's International. Since 1979, I have been very active and have held a variety of chapter offices. During the past three years I have served as a district representative and officer.

Hobbies and Interests:

I enjoy physical exercise (running and racquetball), sailing, piano, theater, gardening, and gourmet cooking.

References:

Dr. James Smith, Superintendent of Norfolk Public Schools.
Mr. Robert Sinclair, Principal, Norfolk High School.
Mr. Paul Amos, Governor, Tidewater District, Toastmasters International.

IMPROVED CHRONOLOGICAL RESUME

KAREN JONES
1234 Main Street
Norfolk, VA 23508
804/440-4321

OBJECTIVE: A public relations position involving program planning and coordination which requires an ability to work with diverse publics, develop publicity and promotional campaigns, market services and benefits, and meet deadlines.

WORK EXPERIENCE:

English Teacher: Norfolk Public Schools, Norfolk, VA.
Taught creative writing and composition. Organized and supervised numerous fund-raising projects which involved local businesses, media, parents, and students. Co-directed senior class plays. Wrote and gave several "keynote" speeches at special student programs. Served as school liaison to Parent-Teachers Association; designed a plan to increase membership and involve parents in school activities. Chaired city-wide public relations committee; coordinated development and production of promotional materials. Served as speech "ghost-writer" and editor for administrators. (1980 to present)

English Teacher: Chesapeake Public Schools, Chesapeake, VA.
Taught English composition. Wrote, designed, and developed multi-media instructional programs to interest students in writing. Served as advisor to student newspaper. (1973-1975)

ADDITIONAL EXPERIENCE:

Toastmasters International, Tidewater Chapter, VA.

District Representative: Elected to governing board of Southeast Virginia District. Served in liaison capacity between district officers and local chapter. Planned, organized, and publicized training workshops and regional competition. (1986 to present).

Chapter Officer (President, Treasurer, Sergeant-at-Arms):
Developed a publicity plan which increased membership by 20 percent. Kept financial records and prepared budget reports. Acquired extensive public speaking experience and training. (1982-1989)

EDUCATION:

M.S.Ed. in Secondary Education, 1979: Old Dominion University, Norfolk, VA
B.A. in English Literature, 1974: University of Virginia, Charlottesville, VA

FUNCTIONAL RESUME

KAREN JONES
1234 Main Street
Norfolk, VA 23508
804/440-4321

OBJECTIVE: A public relations position involving program planning and coordination which requires an ability to work with diverse publics, develop publicity and promotional campaigns, market services and benefits, and meet deadlines.

AREAS OF EFFECTIVENESS

PLANNING AND COORDINATING
Organized and supervised several fund raising projects. Designed and implemented membership campaigns. Chaired public relations committee for school system; coordinated development and production of promotional materials. Publicized special events and programs to constituent groups. Developed multi-media instructional package to facilitate learning and involve students. Taught creative writing.

PROMOTING PUBLICIZING, MARKETING, AND WRITING
Developed promotional plan to attract new members to organizations. Coordinated publicity of special events and media. Wrote and edited speeches for self and school administrators. Helped design and produce promotional materials. Publicized special events and programs to constituent groups. Developed multi-media instructional package to facilitate learning and involve students. Taught creative writing.

COMMUNICATING AND INSTRUCTING
Gave numerous speeches over a seven year period to a variety of audiences. Conducted meetings and chaired committees. Coached administrators in writing and presenting speeches. Taught English for ten years in public schools.

EDUCATION: M.S.Ed., Old Dominion University, Norfolk, VA, 1979.
B.A., University of Virginia, Charlottesville, VA, 1974.

COMBINATION RESUME

KAREN JONES
1234 Main Street
Norfolk, VA 23508
804/440-4321

OBJECTIVE: A public relations position involving program planning and coordination which requires an ability to work with diverse publics, develop publicity and promotional campaigns, market services and benefits, and meet deadlines.

AREAS OF EFFECTIVENESS

**PLANNING
COORDINATING**

Organized and supervised several fund raising projects. Designed and implemented membership campaigns. Chaired public relations committee for school system; coordinated development and production of promotional materials. Publicized special events and programs to constituent groups. Developed multi-media instructional package to facilitate learning and involve students. Taught creative writing.

**PROMOTING
PUBLICIZING,
MARKETING,
AND WRITING**

Developed promotional plan to attract new members to organizations. Coordinated publicity of special events and media. Wrote and edited speeches for self and school administrators. Helped design and produce promotional materials. Publicized special events and programs to constituent groups. Developed multi-media instructional package to facilitate learning and involve students. Taught creative writing.

**COMMUNICATING
AND
INSTRUCTING**

Gave numerous speeches over a seven year period to a variety of audiences. Conducted meetings and chaired committees. Coached administrators in writing and presenting speeches. Taught English for ten years in public schools.

WORK EXPERIENCE:

English Teacher: Norfolk Public Schools, Norfolk, VA.
Taught 11th and 12th grade creative writing and composition. (1980-present)

English Teacher: Chesapeake Public Schools, Chesapeake, VA.
Taught 10th and 11th grade composition. Advisor to student newspaper. (1973-1975).

EDUCATION:

M.S.Ed., Old Dominion University, Norfolk, VA, 1979.
B.A., University of Virginia, Charlottesville, VA, 1974.

RESUME LETTER

1234 Main Street
Norfolk, VA 23508
April 30, 199___

Mr. Dale Roberts
Business Manager
Virginia Beach Convention Center
Virginia Beach, VA 23519

Dear Mr. Roberts:

A mutual acquaintance of ours, Paul Amos, suggested that I contact you about the new Virginia Beach Convention Center. He remarked that you are developing a comprehensive public relations and marketing plan to attract convention business.

As an officer of my local chapter and regional division of Toastmasters International, I have acquired a substantial amount of public relations, special events planning, and program coordination experience. Along with my professional work, my background includes working with diverse audiences, developing publicity campaign and promotional materials, marketing services and benefits, recruiting new members, handling financial records, and meeting important deadlines. Furthermore, I have experience in writing and giving speeches, chairing work groups, representing organizations, creative writing, and teaching.

Since I have a strong interest in public relations-type activities and have a thorough knowledge of our region and its resources, I was quite interested to hear that your new marketing plan may use conference coordinators to work with your sales staff. I would be very interested in learning more about your plans and exploring future possibilities.

I plan to be near your office next week and wonder if we could have a brief meeting? I'll give your office a call in the next few days to see if a mutually convenient time could be arranged.

Sincerely,

Karen Jones

JAMES C. ASTOR

Our third set of examples follows a similar pattern—transforming a Traditional Chronological Resume into Improved Chronological, Functional, Combination, and Letter resumes. In this case, the individual has a background in counseling and training. He seeks to move from public sector employment to a private firm. He was actually terminated from his last government job due to budgetary cutbacks that eliminated his position. This is the first time he has had to write a one-page resume appropriate for the private sector—and he manages to incorporate numerous errors associated with resume writing.

Notice, again, how we take what is essentially a weak self-centered resume filled with potential negatives and transform it into a coherent resume. The new resumes incorporate the individual's major skills and accomplishments as well as target them toward the needs of employers. Take special note of the Combination Resume example. Here we extend the basic one-page resume to a second "Supplemental Information" page. This is a good alternative to writing a two-page resume. The "Supplemental Information" page summarizes major achievements that are best pulled together in this format rather than incorporated into the "Experience" section of the first page.

TRADITIONAL CHRONOLOGICAL RESUME

RESUME

James C. Astor	Weight:	190 lbs.
4921 Taylor Drive	Height:	6'0"
Washington, D.C. 20011	Born:	June 2, 1954
	Health:	Good
	Marital Status:	Divorced

EDUCATION

1983-1984:   M.A., Vocational Counseling, Virginia Commonwealth University, Richmond, Virginia.

1972-1976:   B.A., Psychology, Roanoke College, Salem, Virginia.

1968-1972:   High School Diploma, Richmond Community High School, Richmond, Virginia.

WORK EXPERIENCE

6/13/84 to 8/22/91: Supervisory Trainer, GS-12, U.S. Department of Labor, Washington, D.C. Responsible for all aspects of training. Terminated because of budget cuts.

9/10/82 to 11/21/83: Bartender, Johnnie's Disco, Richmond, Virginia. Part-time while attending college.

4/3/80 to 6/2/82; Counselor, Virginia Employment Commission, Richmond, Virginia. Responsible for interviewing unemployed for jobs. Resigned to work full-time on Master's degree.

8/15/77 to 6/15/79: Guidance counselor and teacher, Petersburg Junior High School, Petersburg, Virginia.

2/11/75 to 10/6/75: Cook and Waiter, Big Mama's Pizza Parlor, Roanoke, Virginia. Part-time while attending college.

PROFESSIONAL AFFILIATIONS

American Personnel and Guidance Association
American Society for Training and Development
Personnel Management Association
Phi Delta Pi

HOBBIES

I like to play tennis, bicycle, and hike.

REFERENCES

David Ryan, Chief, Training Division, U.S. Department of Labor, Washington, D.C. 20012, (202) 735-0121.

Dr. Sara Thomas, Professor, Department of Psychology, George Washington University, Washington, D.C. 20030, (201) 621-4545.

Thomas V. Grant, Area Manager, Virginia Employment Commission, Richmond, Virginia 26412, (804) 261-4089

IMPROVED CHRONOLOGICAL RESUME

JAMES C. ASTOR
4921 Tyler Drive
Washington, DC 20011   212/422-8764

OBJECTIVE: A training and counseling position with a computer firm, where strong administrative, communication, and planning abilities will be used for improving the work performance and job satisfaction of employees.

EXPERIENCE: **U.S. Department of Labor, Washington, DC**
Planned and organized counseling programs for 5,000 employees. Developed training manuals and conducted workshops on interpersonal skills, stress management, and career planning; resulted in a 50 percent decrease in absenteeism. Supervised team of five instructors and counselors. Conducted individual counseling and referrals to community organizations. Advised government agencies and private firms on establishing in-house employee counseling and career development programs. Consistently evaluated as outstanding by supervisors and workshop participants. 1984 to present.

Virginia Employment Commission, Richmond, VA
Conducted all aspects of employment counseling. Interviewed, screened, and counseled 2,500 jobseekers. referred clients to employers and other agencies. Coordinated job vacancy and training information for businesses, industries, and schools. Reorganized interviewing and screening processes which improved the efficiency of operations by 50 percent. Cited in annual evaluation for "outstanding contributions to improving relations with employers and clients." 1980-1982.

Petersburg Junior High School, Petersburg, VA
Guidance counselor for 800 students. Developed program of individualized and group counseling. Taught special social science classes for socially maladjusted and slow learners. 1977-1979.

EDUCATION: M.A., Vocational Counseling, Virginia Commonwealth University, Richmond, VA, 1984.

B.A., Psychology, Roanoke College, Salem, VA, 1976.

REFERENCES: Available upon request.

FUNCTIONAL RESUME

JAMES C. ASTOR

| 4921 Tyler Drive | Washington, DC 20011 | 212/422-8764 |

OBJECTIVE: A training and counseling position with a computer firm, where strong administrative, communication, and planning abilities will be used for improving the work performance and job satisfaction of employees.

EDUCATION: Ph.D. in process, Industrial Psychology, George Washington University, Washington, DC

M.A., Vocational Counseling, Virginia Commonwealth University, Richmond, VA, 1984.

B.A., Psychology, Roanoke College, Salem, VA, 1976.

AREAS OF EFFECTIVENESS:

Administration

Supervised instructors and counselors. Coordinated job vacancy and training information for businesses, industries, and schools.

Communication

Conducted over 100 workshops on interpersonal skills, stress management, and career planning. Frequent guest speaker to various agencies and private firms. Experienced writer of training manuals and public relations materials.

Planning

Planned and developed counseling programs for 5,000 employees. Reorganized interviewing and screening processes for public employment agency. Developed program of individualized and group counseling for community school.

PERSONAL: Enjoy challenges and working with people. . .interested in productivity. . .willing to relocate and travel.

REFERENCES: Available upon request.

COMBINATION RESUME

JAMES C. ASTOR
4921 Tyler Drive
Washington, DC 20011   212/422-8764

OBJECTIVE:	A training and counseling position with a computer firm, where strong administrative, communication, and planning abilities will be used for improving the work performance and job satisfaction of employees.

AREAS OF EFFECTIVENESS

ADMINISTRATION:	Supervised instructors and counselors. Coordinated job vacancy and training information for businesses, industries, and schools.
COMMUNICATION:	Conducted over 100 workshops on interpersonal skills, stress management, and career planning. Frequent guest speaker to various agencies and private firms. Experienced writer of training manuals and public relations materials.
PLANNING:	Planned and developed counseling programs for 5,000 employees. Reorganized interviewing and screening processes for public employment agency. Developed program of individualized and group counseling for community school.
WORK HISTORY:	Supervisory Trainer, U.S. Department of Labor, Washington, DC, 1984 to present.
	Counselor, Virginia Employment Commission, Richmond, VA, 1980-1982.
	Guidance counselor and teacher, Petersburg Junior High School, Petersburg, VA, 1977-1979.
EDUCATION:	M.A., Vocational Counseling, Virginia Commonwealth University, Richmond, VA, 1984.
	B.A., Psychology, Roanoke College, Salem, VA, 1976.
PERSONAL:	Enjoy challenges and working with people. . .interested in productivity. . .willing to relocate and travel.

SUPPLEMENTAL INFORMATION   **JAMES C. ASTOR**

Continuing Education and Training

- Completed 12 semester hours of computer science courses.
- Attended several workshops during past three years on employee counseling and administrative methods:

    "Career Development for Technical Personnel," Professional Management Association, 3 days, 1990.

    "Effective Supervisory Methods for Training Directors," National Training Associates, 3 days, 1989.

    "Training the Trainer," American Society for Training and Development, 3 days, 1988.

    "Time Management," U.S. Department of Labor, 3 days, 1987.

    "Counseling the Substance Abuse Employee," American Management Association, 3 days, 1986.

Training Manuals Developed

- "Managing Employee Stress," U.S. Department of Labor, 1988.
- "Effective Interpersonal Communication in the Workplace," U.S. Department of Labor, 1986.
- "Planning Careers Within the Organization," U.S. Department of Labor, 1985.

Research Projects Completed

- "Employment Counseling Programs for Technical Personnel," U.S. Development of Labor, 1990. Incorporated into agency report on "New Directions in Employee Counseling."
- "Developing Training Programs for Problem Employees," M.A. thesis, Virginia Commonwealth University, 1984.

Professional Affiliations

- American Personnel and Guidance Association
- American Society for Training and Development
- Personnel Management Association

Educational Highlights

- Completing Ph.D. in Industrial Psychology, George Washington University, Washington, D.C. 1992.
- Earned 4.0/4.0 grade point average as graduate student.
- Organized the Graduate Student Counseling Association for George Washington University, 1989.

RESUME LETTER

4921 Tyler Drive
Washington, DC 20011
March 15, 199___

Doris Stevens
STR Corporation
179 South Trail
Rockville, MD 21101

Dear Ms. Stevens:

STR Corporation is one of the most dynamic computer companies in the nation. In addition to being a leader in the field of small business computers, STR has a progressive employee training and development program which could very well become a model for other organizations. This is the type of organization I am interested in joining.

I am seeking a training position with a computer firm which would use my administrative, communication, and planning abilities to develop effective training and counseling programs. My experience includes:

Administration: Supervised instructors and counselors. Coordinated job vacancy and training information for businesses, industries, and schools.

Communication: Conducted over 100 workshops on interpersonal skills, stress management, and career planning. Frequent guest speaker to various agencies and private firms. Experienced writer of training manuals and public relations materials.

Planning: Planned and developed counseling programs for 5,000 employees. Reorganized interviewing and screening processes for public employment agency. Developed program of individualized and group counseling for community school.

In addition, I am completing my Ph.D. in industrial psychology with emphasis on developing training and counseling programs for technical personnel.

Could we meet to discuss your program as well as how my experience might relate to your needs? I will call your office on Tuesday morning, March 23, to arrange a convenient time to meet with you.

I especially want to share with you a model employee counseling and career development program I recently developed. Perhaps you may find it useful for your work with STR.

Sincerely,

James Astor

GEORGE WILLINGTON

Because of our international work, we receive numerous inquiries from individuals who seek international employment. Some individuals have many years of experience working abroad. Others wish to re-enter the international job market after a lengthy absence. And others wish to break into this job market with little or no experience nor marketable international skills. Unfortunately, we hear from a disproportionate number of individuals who are high on motivation to work abroad but very low on international skills and experience and knowledge of international employers and jobs. Many are construction workers who have unrealistic expectations about the marketability of their skills abroad. Indeed, this is the job market for many dreamers who see themselves making tons of money working in some exotic location. It is also a job market for individuals who seriously pursue international careers based upon a sound understanding of the realities of the international job market. In either case, they need a resume that best communicates their qualifications to international employers.

The final set of resume transformation examples are different from the previous examples. Here we show how to change an objective for two different employment arenas—international and domestic—as well as how to move from a self-employed situation to that of employee in someone else's organization. It incorporates the interests of a talented individual who is interested in pursuing many different professional and personal interests which cannot be accommodated in a single job. While he may appear to lack a clear focus—doesn't seem to know what he wants to do—he really wants to do many different things, all of which present new career challenges. So he takes it one job at a time. Whichever job falls in line will be the one he will enjoy.

This individual has a strong professional background in both architecture and construction as well as a personal interest in international travel and work. He also has an interesting personal/professional background that includes technical and writing skills and travel/relocation interests— interesting enough to be included in "Additional Skills and Experience" and "Personal" sections. These additional skills and interests give his resume personality. They set him apart from many other applicants. In the end, they may be the real reason employers invite him to interviews.

Most of George Willington's experience is as an independent contractor rather than as an employee in someone else's organization. He's interested in using his professional skills in either the United States or abroad. However, if he is to appear qualified for an international position, he needs to develop an international objective and then relate his international experience and patterns of achievement to that objective. Notice how we attempt to make this international linkage in the case of an individual with little international work experience.

In the second example, this same individual seeks a building inspection position in a very tight job market related to his architecture and construction skills. This is the first resume this individual has ever written. The resume represents a significant career change—from an independent contractor to a salaried employee. In making this career change, George Willington presents his skills as **patterns of accomplishments** related to his architectural and construction experience.

The third example could be used for either a domestic or international position. Here the objective is generic enough to be used with a variety of different employers. We've also elaborated more on the "Project Management" experience section since this is his strongest skill and it reinforces the objective.

The outcome of these three different resumes is that George Willington acquired an exciting and flexible building inspection position which could eventually lead to some international work. It also allows him to pursue several other professional and personal interests. The job represents an excellent "fit" with his on-going and evolving professional skills and personal interests. He's using the skills he most enjoys using as well as acquiring new knowledge and experience in both the architectural and construction fields.

GEORGE WILLINGTON
1131 N. Bridge Road
Baltimore, MD 21027
301/111-0000

OBJECTIVE: An overseas construction management/supervision position with an international design/build firm.

EDUCATION: New York Institute of Technology
Albany, New York
Bachelor of Architecture, 1977

Technische Universitat Hannover, Doctoral Program
Hanover, Germany
World Student Fund Fellowship, 1979

AREAS OF EFFECTIVENESS

MANAGEMENT: Owner and President for 14 years of a design/build firm with annual revenues between 1 and 2 million.

CONSTRUCTION: Direct experience with most methodologies of construction including wood frame, masonry, and light metal.

SUPERVISION: Responsible for 15 full-time employees. Concurrently supervised several hundred sub-contractors/crews. Many crews were non-English speaking.

ARCHITECTURAL DESIGN:
- Residential experience with custom and track family homes ranging from 1000 to 10,000 square feet.

- Commercial experience with retail, office, office/warehouse, warehouse, restaurants, and marinas.

OVERSEAS:
- Fluent in German, written and spoken.

- Experienced working, researching, and residing abroad—11 years in northern Europe and several Third World countries.

COMMUNITY: President of Western Maryland Building Industries Association, an affiliate of The National Association of Home Builders.

ADDITIONAL SKILLS AND EXPERIENCE:
- Computer Proficient (including Acad)
- P-IFR Pilot
- U.S. Coast Guard Commercial Captains License
- Ham Radio Operator
- Co-author of 3 books

PERSONAL: 37, single, excellent health, enthusiastic to travel and/or relocate for the appropriate challenge.

GEORGE WILLINGTON
1131 N. Bridge Road
Baltimore, MD 21027
301/111-0000

OBJECTIVE: A building inspection position involving all phases of both
                 residential and commercial construction.

EDUCATION: New York Institute of Technology
                 Albany, New York
                 Bachelor of Architecture, 1977

                 Technische Universitat Hannover, Doctoral Program
                 Hanover, Germany
                 World Student Fund Fellowship, 1979

                 AREAS OF EFFECTIVENESS

MANAGEMENT: Owner and President for 14 years of a design/build firm with
                 annual revenues between 1 and 2 million.

CONSTRUCTION: Direct experience with most methodologies of construction
                 including wood frame, masonry, and light metal.

SUPERVISION: Responsible for 15 full-time employees. Concurrently super-
                 vised several hundred sub-contractors/crews.

ARCHITECTURAL   • Residential experience with custom and tract family homes,
DESIGN: ranging from 1000 to 10,000 square feet.

                 • Commercial experience with retail, office, office/warehouse,
                   warehouse, restaurants, and marinas.

COMMUNITY: President of Western Maryland Building Industries
                 Association, an affiliate of The National Association
                 of Home Builders.

ADDITIONAL   • Computer Proficient (including Acad)
SKILLS AND   • P-IFR Pilot
EXPERIENCE: • U.S. Coast Guard Commercial Captains License
                • Ham Radio Operator
                • Co-author of 3 books

PERSONAL: 37, excellent health, willing to travel and/or relocate for the
                 appropriate challenge.

GEORGE WILLINGTON
1131 N. Bridge Road
Baltimore, MD 21027
301/111-0000

OBJECTIVE:	A construction/contract management position on a multi-faceted project requiring strong managerial, scheduling, and supervisory skills.
EDUCATION:	New York Institute of Technology Albany, New York Bachelor of Architecture, 1977
	Technische Universitat Hannover, Doctoral Program Hanover, Germany World Student Fund Fellowship, 1979

AREAS OF EFFECTIVENESS

PROJECT MANAGEMENT:	Owner and President for 14 years of a multi-million dollar design/build firm. Involved in all phases of project management, including contract negotiations, change order administration, scheduling, and personnel.
CONSTRUCTION:	Direct experience with most methodologies of construction including wood frame, masonry, and light metal.
SUPERVISION:	Responsible for 15 full-time employees. Concurrently supervised several hundred sub-contractors/crews.
ARCHITECTURAL DESIGN:	• Residential experience with custom and tract family homes, ranging from 1000 to 10,000 square feet. • Commercial experience with retail, office, office/warehouse, warehouse, restaurants, and marinas.
OVERSEAS:	• Fluent in German, written and spoken. • Experienced working, researching, and residing abroad—11 years in northern Europe and several Third World countries.
COMMUNITY:	President of Western Maryland Building Industries Association, an affiliate of The National Association of Home Builders.
ADDITIONAL SKILLS AND EXPERIENCE:	• Computer Proficient (including Acad) • P-IFR Pilot • U.S. Coast Guard Commercial Captains License • Ham Radio Operator • Co-author of 3 books
PERSONAL:	37, excellent health, willing to travel and/or relocate for the appropriate challenge.

Chapter Six

RESUME EXAMPLES

The resume examples in this final chapter illustrate different educational, experience, and occupational levels. Each resume follows the principles outlined in previous chapters.

The resumes on pages 117-121 reflect different educational and experience levels. The resume on page 117, for example, is for a high school graduate with vocational skills and experience. The resume on page 118 is for a junior college graduate with a non-traditional background. The resume on page 119 is appropriate for a recent B.A. graduate.

The example on pages 119-120 differs from all others. Especially appropriate for individuals with an M.A. or Ph.D. degree, or for those with specialized research, publication, and other production experience, this example includes an add-on supplemental sheet which lists relevant qualifications. The main resume is still one page. The add-on sheet is designed to reinforce the major thrust of the resume without distracting from it. This is an ideal resume for someone who needs to include examples of their work within the framework of the one to two-page resume.

The remaining resumes in this chapter represent different occupations and positions such as accounting, attorney, bookkeeping, computers, construction, financial analyst, paralegal, publishing, and sales. It also includes examples using a "Summary of Qualifications" and a two-page resume.

JOHN ALBERT
1099 Seventh Avenue
Akron, OH 44522
322/645-8271

OBJECTIVE: **A position as architectural drafter** with a firm specializing in commercial construction where technical knowledge and practical experience will enhance construction design and building operations.

EXPERIENCE: <u>**Draftsman:**</u> Akron Construction Company, Akron, OH. Helped develop construction plans for $14 million of residential and commercial construction. (1985 to present).

<u>**Cabinet Maker:**</u> Jason's Linoleum and Carpet Company, Akron, OH. Designed and constructed kitchen counter tops and cabinets; installed the material in homes; cut and laid linoleum flooring in apartment complexes. (1982 to 1985).

<u>**Carpenter's Assistant:**</u> Kennison Associates, Akron, OH. Assisted carpenter in the reconstruction of a restaurant and in building of forms for pouring concrete. (Summer 1981).

<u>**Materials Control Auditor:**</u> Taylor Machine and Foundry, Akron, OH. Collected data on the amount of material being utilized daily in the operation of the foundry. Evaluated the information to determine the amount of materials being wasted. Submitted reports to production supervisor on the analysis of weekly and monthly production. (Summer 1980)

TRAINING: <u>**Drafting School, Akron Vocational and Technical Center**</u>, 1984. Completed 15 months of training in drafting night school.

EDUCATION: <u>**Akron Community High School**</u>, Akron, OH. Graduated in 1983.

PERSONAL: 25...single...willing to relocate...prefer working both indoors and outdoors...strive for perfection...hard worker...enjoy photography, landscaping, furniture design and construction.

REFERENCES: Available upon request.

GARY S. PLATT
2238 South Olby Road, Sacramento, CA 97342
712/564-3981

OBJECTIVE

A position in the areas of systems analysis and implementation of Management Information Systems which will utilize a demonstrated ability to improve systems performance. Willing to relocate.

RELATED EXPERIENCE

Engineering Technician, U.S. Navy.
Reviewed technical publications to improve operational and technical descriptions and maintenance procedures. Developed system operation training course for high-level, nontechnical managers. Developed PERT charts for scheduling 18-month overhauls. Installed and checked out digital computer equipment with engineers. Devised and implemented a planned maintenance program and schedule for computer complex to reduce equipment down-time and increase utilization by user departments. (1986 to present)

Assistant Manager/System Technician, U.S. Navy, 37 person division.
Established and coordinated preventive/corrective maintenance system for four missile guidance systems (9 work centers) resulting in increased reliability. Advised management on system operation and utilization for maximum effectiveness. Performed system test analysis and directed corrective maintenance actions. Interfaced with other managers to coordinate interaction of equipment and personnel. Conducted maintenance and safety inspections of various types of work centers. (1982 to 1985)

Assistant Manager/System Technician, U.S. Navy, 25 person division.
Supervised system tests, analyzed results, and directed maintenance actions on two missile guidance systems. Overhauled and adjusted within factory specifications two special purpose computers, reducing down-time over 50%. Established and coordinated system and computer training program. During this period, both systems received the "Battle Efficiency E For Excellence" award in competition with others units. (1979 to 1981)

EDUCATION

U.S. Navy Schools, 1984-1988:
Digital System Fundamentals, Analog/Digital Digital/Analog Conversion Techniques, UNIVAC 1219B Computer Programming, and Technical Writing.

A.S. in Education, June 1982:
San Diego Community College, San Diego, CA
Highlight:
>Graduated Magna Cum Laude
>Member, Phi Beta Kappa Honor Society

CHERYL AYERS
2589 Jason Drive
Ithaca, NY 14850

202/467-8735

OBJECTIVE: A research, data analysis, and planning position in law enforcement administration which will use leadership, responsibility, and organizational skills for improving the efficiency of operations.

EDUCATION: <u>B.S. in Criminal Justice</u>, 1991
Ithaca College, Ithaca, NY
- Major: Law Enforcement Administration
- Minor: Management Information Systems
  G.P.A. in concentration 3.6/4.0

AREAS OF EFFECTIVENESS:

<u>Leadership</u>
Head secretary while working at State Police.
Served as Rush Chair and Social Chair for Chi Phi Sorority.
Elected Captain and Co-Captain three times during ten years of cheerleading.

<u>Responsibility</u>
Handled highly confidential information, material, and files for State Police.
Aided in the implementation of on-line banking system.
In charge of receiving and dispersing cash funds for drive-in restaurant.

<u>Organization</u>
Revised ticket system for investigators' reports at State Police.
Planning schedules and budget, developed party themes and skits, obtained prop material, and delegated and coordinated work of others during sorority rush.

<u>Data Analysis</u>
Program in Fortran, Cobal, and RPG II.
Analyzed State Police data on apprehensions; wrote report.

PERSONAL: 22...excellent health...single...enjoy all sports and challenges...willing to relocate.

REFERENCES: Available upon request from the Office of Career Planning and Placement, Ithaca College, Ithaca, NY

MICHELE R. FOLGER
733 Main Street
Williamsburg, VA 23572
804/376-9932

OBJECTIVE: A manager/practitioner position in public relations which will use research, writing, and program experience. Willing to relocate.

EXPERIENCE: **Program Development**
Conducted research on the representation of minority students in medical colleges. Developed proposal for a major study in the field. Secured funding for $845,000 project. Coordinated and administered the program which had major effect on medical education.

Initiated and developed a national minority student recruitment program for 20 medical colleges.

Writing
Compiled and published reports in a variety of educational areas. Produced several booklets on urban problems for general distribution. Published articles in professional journals. Wrote and presented conference papers.

Research
Gathered and analyzed information concerning higher education in a variety of specialized fields. Familiar with data collection and statistics. Good knowledge of computers.

Administration and Management
Hired and trained research assistants. Managed medium-sized office and supervised 30 employees.

Public Relations
Prepared press releases and conducted press conferences. Organized and hosted receptions and social events. Spoke to various civic, business, and professional organizations.

WORK HISTORY: ATS Research Associates, Washington, DC
Virginia Education Foundation, Richmond, VA
Eaton's Advertising Agency, Cincinnati, OH

EDUCATION: M.A., Journalism, College of William and Mary, 1987.
B.A., English Literature, University of Cincinnati, 1981.

REFERENCES: Available upon request.

SUPPLEMENTAL INFORMATION   MICHELE R. FOLGER

Public Speaking

- "The New Public Relations," New York Public Relations Society, New York City, April 8, 1991.
- "How to Prepare an Effective Press Conference," Virginia Department of Public Relations, Richmond, Virginia, November 21, 1990.
- "New Approaches to Public Relations," United States Chamber of Commerce, Washington, D.C., February 26, 1990.

Professional Activities

- Delegate, State Writer's Conference, Roanoke, VA, 1991.
- Chair, Journalism Club, College of William and Mary, 1990.
- Secretary, Creative Writing Society, University of Cincinnati, 1989.
- Co-Chair, Public Relations in the United States Conference, College of William and Mary, 1989.
- Chair, Women's Conference, Junior League of Cincinnati, 1988.

Publications

- "The Creative Writer Today," Times Literary, Vol. 6, No. 3 (September 1990), pp. 34-51.
- "Representation of Minority Medical Students," Medical Education, Vol. 32, No. 1 (January 1990), pp. 206-218.
- "Recruiting Minority Students to Medical Colleges in the Northeast," Medical College Bulletin, Vol. 23, No. 4 (March 1989), pp. 21/29.

Reports

- "Increasing Representation of Minority Students in 50 Medical Colleges," submitted to the Foundation for Medical Education, Washington, DC, May 1990, 288 pages.
- "Urban Education as a Problem of Urban Decay," submitted to the Urban Education Foundation, New York City, September 1989, 421 pages.

Continuing Education

- "Grantsmanship Workshop," Williamsburg, Virginia, 1989.
- "Developing Public Relations Writing Skills," workshop, Washington, D.C., 1989.
- "New Program Development Approaches for the 1980's," Virginia Beach, Virginia, 1985.
- "Research Design and Data Analysis in the Humanities," University of Michigan, 1987.

Educational Highlights

- Assistant Editor of the Literary Times, University of Cincinnati, 1984-1985.
- Earned 3.8/4.0 grade point average as undergraduate and 4.0/4.0 as graduate student while working full time.
- M.A. Thesis: "Creating Writing Approaches to Public Relations."

PUBLISHING/COMPUTERS

MARY FURNISS
7812 W. 24th St.   821/879-1124
Dallas, TX 71234

OBJECTIVE:	**A management position** involving the application of computer technology for improving the efficiency of publishing operations.
EXPERIENCE:	<u>**Computer Applications Manager, 1989 to present**</u> Stevens Publishing Company, Fort Worth, TX Managed all computer-related projects for publishing firm with annual sales of $40 million. Presented yearly capital expenditure and general systems budget, negotiated computer service contracts, evaluated and recommended new equipment and software purchases, and trained staff to use software and hardware. Replaced ATEX typesetting with desktop publishing system that immediately saved the company $650,000 in operational costs. <u>**Editorial/Production Supervisor, 1986-1988**</u> Benton Publishing Company, San Francisco, CA Supervised all computer-related projects. Trained staff of 27 to use WordPerfect and other software applications. Devised an innovative system that transformed traditional galley editing into an efficient electronic editing system. New computerized system eliminated the need for two additional employees to handle the traditional galley editing system. Reduced errors by 70 percent. <u>**Editorial Assistant, 1984-1985**</u> Benton Publishing Company, San Francisco, CA Prepared annual *Encyclopedia of International Forestry* materials for editing and production. Supervised freelancers for special editorial projects. Proofread and copy-edited materials for 18 books produced annually. Received "Employee of the Year" award for initiating a new computerized editing system that saved the company $70,000 in annual freelance editing fees.
EDUCATION:	<u>University of Washington</u> B.A., Journalism, 1984.
SPECIAL SKILLS:	Familiar with the ATEX typesetting system and the application of Ventura desktop publishing software. Attended two advanced training programs in the use of computerized editing systems.
PERSONAL:	Enjoy developing innovative and cost-saving approaches to traditional publishing tasks that involve the application of computer technology. Work well in team settings and with training groups. Willing to relocate for the appropriate challenge.

CONSTRUCTION/PROJECT MANAGER

JAMES BARSTOW
7781 West Gate Road
Cincinnati, OH 44411

421/827-0841

OBJECTIVE

A challenging project manager position involving all phases of construction where a demonstrated record of timely and cost-effective completion of projects is important to both the company and its clients.

SUMMARY OF QUALIFICATIONS

- 28 years of progressively responsible construction management experience involving all facets of construction, from start-up to final inspection.
- Experienced in supervising all aspects of construction including masonry, concrete work, carpentry, electrical, mechanical, and plumbing.
- Communicate and work well with individuals at all levels from client to architect to subcontractors.

EXPERIENCE

Independent Contractor, Barstow & Thomas, Cincinnati, OH

Owned and managed a general contracting company doing $8 million in commercial construction each year. Performed all estimating, established contacts with subcontractors, purchased specialty items and materials, and handled shop drawings. Managed all time scheduling, monthly and submonthly draws, and guaranties. Hired all superintendents. Completed most jobs within 30 days of projected completion dates and managed to keep costs 5 percent under estimates. 1981 to 1992.

Job Superintendent, J.P. Snow, Columbus, OH

Supervised all work from start-up to final inspection as well as established all time schedules from start to finish. Handled shop drawings, lab testing, job testing, change orders, daily reports, job progress reports, payroll, and hiring. Worked with client, architect, and city, state, and federal inspectors. Responsible for all concrete and carpentry work including piers, beams, slabs, paving, walls, curbs, and walkways. Initiated an innovative scheduling system that saved the employer more than $60,000 in projected down-time. Consistently praised for taking initiative, providing exceptional leadership, and communicating well with clients, architects, and subcontactors. 1971-1980.

Subcontractor, Smith & Company, Columbus, OH

Conducted all bidding, estimating, and purchasing for more than 50 commercial masonry projects. Worked with both union and open shop help. Managed payroll for 75 employees during different project phases. Projects included hospitals, churches, schools, office buildings, and retail shops. 1967-1970.

ACCOUNTANT

MARY SOUTHERN
721 James Court
Chicago, IL 60029   401/281-9472

OBJECTIVE: **An accounting/finance position** where analytic and
computer skills will be used for managing major accounts
and acquiring new corporate clientele.

EXPERIENCE: <u>Accountant, J.S. Conners & Co., Chicago, IL</u>
Analyzed accounting systems and installed new IBM
ledger system for over 30 corporate accounts. Conducted
training programs attended by more than 500 accountants
with small businesses. Developed proposals, presented
demonstration programs, and prepared reports for
corporate clients. Increased new accounts by 42% over a
four year period. 1987 to present.

<u>Junior Accountant, Simon Electrical Co., Chicago, IL</u>
Acquired extensive experience in all aspects of corporate
accounting while assigned to the Controller's Office.
Prepared detailed financial records for corporate meetings
as well as performed basic accounting tasks such as
journal entries, reconciling discrepancies, and checking
records for accuracy and consistency. Assisted office in
converting to a new computerized accounting system that
eliminated the need for additional personnel and
significantly improved the accuracy and responsiveness.
1983 to 1986.

<u>Accounting Clerk, Johnson Supplies, Chicago, IL</u>
Acquired working knowledge of basic accounting
functions for a 200+ employee organization with annual
revenues of $45 million. Prepared journal vouchers, posted
entries, and completed standard reports. Proposed a
backup accounting system that was implemented by the
Senior Accountant. 1980 to 1982.

EDUCATION: <u>Roosevelt University, Chicago, IL</u>
B.S., Accounting, 1979.
Highlights:
Minor in Computer Science. Worked as a summer
intern with Ballston Accounting Company. Honors
graduate with a 3.7/4.0 GPA in all course work.

REFERENCES: Available upon request.

PARALEGAL

CHARLES DAVIS
771 Anderson Street
Knoxville, TN 37921

421/789-5677

OBJECTIVE:	**A paralegal position** with a firm specializing in criminal law where research and writing skills and an attention to detail will be used for completing timely assignments.
EDUCATION:	**University of Illinois, Champaign, IL** B.A., Criminal Justice, 1991. Highlights: 　　Minor, English 　　President, Paralegal Student Association, 1990. 　　3.7/4.0 GPA **Rock Island Junior College, Rock Island, IL** A.A., English, 1989. **AREAS OF EFFECTIVENESS**
LAW:	Completed 36 semester hours of criminal justice course work with special emphasis on criminal law. Served as an intern with law firm specializing in criminal law. Interviewed clients, drafted documents, conducted legal research, assisted lawyers in preparing court briefs. Participated in criminal justice forums sponsored by the Department of Criminal Justice at the University of Illinois.
RESEARCH:	Conducted research on several criminal cases as both a student and a paralegal intern. Experienced in examining court cases, interviewing lawyers and judges, and observing court proceedings. Proficient in using microfiche and computerized data bases for conducting legal research.
COMMUNICATION:	Prepared research papers, legal summaries, and memos and briefed attorneys on criminal cases relevant to assignments. Used telephone extensively for interviewing clients and conducting legal research.
WORK EXPERIENCE:	**Paralegal Intern, Stanford and Rollins, Peoria, IL.** Summer Intern, 1990. Assigned to numerous research projects relevant to pending criminal cases. **Part-time employment.** Held several part-time positions while attending school full-time. These included student assistant in the Department of Criminal Justice, University of Illinois.

BOOKKEEPER

JANE BARROWS
997 Mountain Road
Denver, CO 80222   717/349-0137

OBJECTIVE: **A manager or assistant manager position** with an
Accounting Department requiring strong supervisory and
communication skills.

EXPERIENCE: <u>**Manager, Accounts Payable, T.L. Dutton, Denver, CO.**</u>
Supervised 18 employees who routinely processed 200
invoices a day. Handled vendor inquiries and adjustments.
Conducted quarterly accruals and reconciliations. Screened
candidates and conducted annual performance evaluations.
Reduced the number of billing errors by 30 percent and
vendor inquiries by 25% within the first year. 1987 to
present.

<u>**Supervisor, Accounts Payable, AAA Pest Control,**</u>
<u>**Denver, CO.**</u>
Supervised 10 employees who processed nearly 140
invoices a day. Audited vendor invoices, authorized
payments, and balanced daily disbursements. Introduced
automated accounts receivable system for improving the
efficiency and accuracy of receivables. 1984 to 1986.

<u>**Bookkeeper, Davis Nursery, Ft. Collins, CO.**</u>
Processed accounts payable and receivable, reconciled
accounts, balanced daily disbursements, and managed
payroll for a 20-employee organization with annual
revenues of $1.8 million. 1981 to 1983.

<u>**Bookkeeper, Jamison's Lumber, Ft Collins, CO.**</u>
Assisted accountant in processing accounts payable and
receivable and managing payroll for a 40-employee
organization with annual revenues of $3.2 million.

EDUCATION: <u>**Colorado Junior College, Denver, CO.**</u>
Currently taking advanced courses in accounting,
computer science, and management.

<u>**Terrance Vo-Tech School, Terrance, CO.**</u>
Completed commercial courses, 1980.

REFERENCES: Available upon request.

FINANCIAL ANALYST

SUSAN ALLEN
325 West End Street
Atlanta, GA 30019   402/378-9771

OBJECTIVE: **A financial analyst position** with a bank where
experience with investment portfolios will be used
for attracting new clientele.

EXPERIENCE: **Investment Analyst, First City Bank, Atlanta, GA.**
Managed $650 million in diverse portfolios for bank's
major clients which averaged 12 percent annual return on
investment. Regularly met with clients, reviewed current
investments, and presented new investment options for
further diversifying portfolios. Introduced biweekly news-
letter for communicating investment strategies with clients
and bank officers. 1988 to 1991.

Research Analyst, Georgia Bank, Atlanta, GA.
Conducted research, wrote reports, and briefed supervisor
on stock market trends and individual companies which
affected the bank's $1.2 billion securities portfolio.
Worked closely with Investment Analyst in developing
new approaches to communicating research findings and
summary reports to clients and bank officers. 1985 to
1987

**Research Assistant/Intern, Columbia Savings Bank,
Columbia, SC.**
Served as a Summer Intern while completing undergraduate degree. Assigned as Research Assistant to Chief Analyst. Followed stock market trends and conducted research
on selected investment banks. 1982.

EDUCATION: **University of Miami, Miami, FL.**
MBA, Business Administration, 1984.
Focused course work on finance and management.
Thesis: "Successful Investment Strategies of Florida's
Ten Major Banks."

University of South Carolina, Columbia, SC.
B.S., Finance, Department of Commerce, 1982.
Summer Intern with Columbia Savings Bank.
Secretary/Treasurer of the Student Business Association.

REFERENCES: Available upon request.

SALES MANAGER

MARK ABLE
7723 Stevens Avenue
Phoenix, AZ 80023   802/461-0921

OBJECTIVE:

A retail management position where demonstrated skills in sales and marketing and enthusiasm for innovation will be used for improving customer service and expanding department profitability.

SUMMARY OF QUALIFICATIONS:

Twelve years of progressively responsible experience in all phases of retail sales and marketing with major discount stores in culturally diverse metropolitan areas. Annually improved profitability by 15 percent and consistently rated in top 10 percent of workforce.

EXPERIENCE:

Sales Manager, K-Mart, Memphis, TN
Managed four departments with annual sales of nearly $8 million. Hired, trained, and supervised a culturally diverse workforce of 14 full-time and 6 part-time employees. Reorganized displays, developed new marketing approaches, coordinated customer feedback with buyers in upgrading quality of merchandize, and improved customer service that resulted in 25 percent increase in annual sales. Received "Outstanding" performance evaluation and "Employee of the Year" award. 1987 to present.

Assistant Buyer, Wal-Mart, Memphis, TN
Maintained inventory levels for three departments with annual sales of $5 million. Developed more competitive system of vendor relations that reduced product costs by 5 percent. Incorporated latest product and merchandizing trends into purchasing decisions. Worked closely with department managers in maintaining adequate inventory levels for best-selling items. 1983 to 1986.

Salesperson, Zayres, Knoxville, TN
Responsible for improving sales in four departments with annual sales of $3.5 million. Reorganized displays and instituted new "Ask An Expert" system for improved customer relations. Sales initiatives resulted in a 20 percent increase in annual sales. Cited for "Excellent customer relations" in annual performance evaluation. Worked part-time while completing education. 1980-1982.

EDUCATION:

University of Tennessee, Knoxville, TN
B.S., Marketing, 1982.
Earned 80 percent of educational expenses while working part-time and maintaining full course loads.

MILITARY/ATTORNEY

STEVEN MARSH
2001 West James Ct.
Seattle, WA 98322

Home: 501/789-4321
Work: 501/789-5539

OBJECTIVE

A position in aviation law where proven management, organization, and supervisory skills and an exceptional record of success in investigating, adjudicating, settling, defending, and prosecuting cases will be used in settling cases to the benefit of employer and clients.

EXPERIENCE

Chief Circuit Defense Counsel, Davis Air Force Base, Ogden, UT
Personally defended all Flying Evaluation Boards (4), winning every one. Successfully defended felony trials covering offenses of drug use, distribution, assault, DUI, and perjury. Supervised, trained, and directed 22 attorneys and 17 paralegals responsible for total defense services across 16 Air Force installations located in 12 states. Included oversight of over 500 trials with every offense up to and including premeditated murder. 1988-1991

Chief, Aviation Settlement Branch, U.S. Air Force, Washington, DC
Directed the investigation, adjudication, and either settlement or litigation of all aviation, environmental, medical malpractice, and other tort claims filed against the Air Force. In 1988, this topped a $40 billion dollar exposure with the percentage of payout to claimed amount the lowest in over a decade. Supervised staff of 13 attorneys and 5 paralegals. Re-formulated U.S. Air Force policy on tort claim and litigation matters in conjunction with the Department of Justice leading to a better concept and application of paying the losers and spending time and resources to win-the-winners. 1986-1987

Chief, Tort Section, U.S. Air Force, Washington, DC
Supervised the investigation and recommended adjudication or litigation of all aviation tort claims against the Air Force, including the last of the Agent Orange cases and the KAL 007 Korean airliner shoot-down by the Soviet Union. Supervised staff of 3 attorneys and 1 paralegal. Recommended U.S. Air Force policy change on aviation tort claims that directly resulted in greater Agency latitude for meritorious claims independent of the previously required GAO Office requirements. 1985

Staff Judge Advocate, Stevens Air Force Base, Miami, FL
Advised top management of all legal issues to include the convening of Aircraft Accident Boards and Flying Evaluation Boards. Directed tort, labor, environmental, procurement, and criminal law procedures. During this period, defended two state environmental Notice of Violations successfully, and over 40 criminal cases were prosecuted without a single acquittal. Served as management's Chief Labor Resolution Negotiator securing settlements at 60 percent of the previously approved maximums. Supervised staff of 4 attorneys and 5 paralegals. 1982-1984

Assistant Staff Judge Advocate, Lowry Air Force Base, CO
Served as government prosecutor for over 35 trials with no acquittals. Served as government representative in over 20 administrative hearings with no losses. Counseled clients on rights/duties under state and federal law. 1978-1981

Area Defense Counsel, Marshall Air Force Base, Austin, TX
Defended over 300 clients in criminal trials, administrative hearings, or minor disciplinary concerns. 1977

Assistant Staff Judge Advocate, Myrtle Beach Air Force Base, SC
Investigated and adjudicated all claims arising from a major B-52 bomber aircraft accident, supervising team of paralegals. Government prosecutor for 12 trials and boards, with zero losses.

EDUCATION

J.D., Boston University College of Law, Boston, MA, 1976
B.A. (Political Science), University of North Carolina, Chapel Hill, NC, 1969

TRAINING

Armed Forces Staff College, Joint Service Program, Residence, 1986
Air War College, USAF, Seminar Program, 1985
Air Command and Staff College, USAF, Seminar Program, 1981
Squadron Officers School, USAF, Residence Program (Dist. Grad.), 1978
Officer Training School, USAF, Residence Program (Dist. Grad.), 1971

AWARDS

Stuart Reichart Award, Senior Attorney, HQ USAF, 1989
Ramirez Award, Outstanding Attorney Tactical Air Command, 1985
Outstanding Attorney, U.S. Air Forces Colorado, 1981

OTHER EXPERIENCE

U.S. Parole Board Hearing Member, USAF, 1989
Joint Services Consolidation Committee, 1985-1986
Navigator and Weapons Officer, U.S. Air Force, F-4 Phantom Aircraft, 100+ sorties, 1973-1975
Police Officer, U.S. Air Force, 1971-1972

BAR MEMBERSHIPS

U.S. Supreme Court, 1989
U.S. Court of Appeals, 4th Circuit, 1985
U.S. Court of Military Appeals, 1979
Supreme Court of Massachusetts, 1976

Chapter Seven

RESUME RESOURCES

Today's marketplace is literally flooded with resume and cover letter books as well as computer software and videos designed to help individuals write better resumes and letters. Indeed, resume books tend to be the first book of choice for many people involved in a job search. Cover letter books have become increasingly popular as more and more individuals recognize the need to improve their letter writing skills along with their resume writing skills.

Any market with a high demand will generate numerous suppliers providing products to satisfy the demand. And like many markets, the resume and letter writing market exhibits many resources of questionable value. In this chapter we examine several of these resources with an eye toward the best quality.

QUESTIONABLE ADVICE, EMBARRASSING EXAMPLES

During the past twelve years we have had an opportunity to review many of these resources. Sad to say, it's a disappointing lot. Nearly 80 percent of the resume books we've encountered get poor marks. Despite authors' claims to being *"professional headhunters," "job search specialists," "professional resume writers," "experienced executives who read or screen hundreds or thousands of resumes each year,"* or keepers of a unique set of resumes that *"really did get jobs,"* we've not been overly impressed. Most writers tend to be unfamiliar with the major career planning and job search literature, perhaps reading only a book or two. Claiming "experience" as their basis for credibility, many are unfamiliar with mainstream career planning and job search methods which are not incorporated in their books. More often than not, they give standard to poor advice and offer what might be best termed embarrassing examples. Indeed, we are surprised to find so many of these "experts" still presenting traditional chronological resumes—complete with height, weight, marital status, sex, age, dates of employment first, duties and responsibilities, and the word "RESUME" firmly planted at the top as examples of resume excellence!

Most example books tend to be compilations of resumes the authors happened to have on hand rather than examples based upon sound principles of effective resume writing. Many are very disorganized—jumping from one unrelated topic to another—lack a clear approach and focus, are outdated, and are anything but user-friendly. Furthermore, many resume books are preoccupied with the writing exercise to the exclusion of such critical how-to processes as resume production, distribution, follow-up, and evaluation. None link resumes to the larger job search process of self-assessment, research, networking, and interviewing.

BOOKS AND THEIR APPROACHES

Resume and letter writing books tend to fall into two general categories-those that primarily emphasize the writing **process** versus those that primarily present **examples**. Most of the process books only address principles of resume writing and production. A few books, such as this one, attempt to **link** the complete process to the examples as well as to the larger job search process. To our surprise, hardly any books address the critical issues of resume distribution, follow-up, and evaluation. This seems strange especially when a book claims to offer examples of "effective resumes." After all, "effectiveness" is not only a function of writing and production; it must include **distribution and follow-up**—the keys to getting resumes read and responded to.

While we've tried to present a user-friendly book oriented towards results, we recognize that *Dynamite Resumes* may not answer all of your questions. Therefore, you may want to examine some other resume books for additional advice and examples. Be forewarned, however, that most of these books primarily focus on writing and production—not distribution, follow-up, and evaluation. We have found the following books to be some of the best resume guides available today. Some are available in your local library or bookstore or they can be ordered directly from Impact Publications by completing the order form at the end of this book.

Asher, Donald, *The Overnight Resume* (Berkeley, CA: Ten Speed Press, 1991, $6.95). Packed with solid tips on how to write a results-oriented resume. One of the better nuts-and-bolts oriented new books on the subject.

Fry, Ronald W., *Your First Resume* (Hawthorne, NJ: Career Press, 1989, $10.95). Designed for the first-time job seeker, this book walks the neophyte resume writer through the major steps in the resume writing, production, and distribution processes. Provides sound advice on resume writing. Includes examples of resumes and letters, some of which were taken from our *High Impact Resumes and Letters* book!

Good, C. Edward, *Does Your Resume Wear Blue Jeans?* (Charlottesville, VA: Blue Jeans Press, 1989, $7.95). Somewhat difficult to find, nonetheless, this is one of the best resume books available today. Well organized and easy-to-read, the book is filled with great tips on resume structure, form, content, and language. The author is a professional writer and expert on grammar who stresses the importance of clear communication. He has authored or co-authored three other resume books tailored to the needs of high school students, women re-entering the job market, and military personnel making career transitions: *Does Your Resume Wear Blue Jeans High School Edition?*, *Does Your Resume Wear Apron Strings?*, and *Does Your Resume Wear Combat*

Boots? He also has produced a two-tape video based upon these books: *Does Your Resume Wear Blue Jeans? Resume Writing Workshop* ($129.95).

Jackson, Tom, *The Perfect Resume* (New York: Doubleday, 1990, $10.95). One of the best resume writing and production books on the market today developed by one of the country's leading career professionals. Walks the user through each step of putting together an effective resume. Based upon sound career planning and job search principles. Includes self-assessment devices, worksheets, and "before" and "after" examples tied to the principles. Uses "Job Target" rather than "Objective" which does not seem to strengthen the resume examples. A computer program system based on this book is also available in different versions for IBM and compatible systems: *Perfect Resume Computer Kit* (Personal—$49.95; Counselor Version—$259.95; Lab Pack—$635.95; Network Version—$995.95).

Kaplan, Robbie Miller, *Sure-Hire Resumes* (New York: AMACOM, 1990, $14.95). Primarily an "example" book with a brief front-end discussion of resume writing principles. This unique book primarily focuses on "resume makeovers"—how to rewrite resumes that are weak or just "average." Includes numerous examples of "before" and "after" resumes with extensive notations on their weak points and how they can be best rescued. Also includes examples of cover letters which are related to specific job vacancy ads.

Krannich, Ronald L. and William J. Banis, *High Impact Resumes and Letters, 4th ed.* (Woodbridge, VA: Impact Publications, 1990, $12.95). Examines the whole process of writing, producing, distributing, following-up and evaluating both resumes and a variety of job search letters. Relates resumes and letters to the larger job search process. Based on sound career planning and job search principles. Strong on the use of self-assessment data for structuring information on the resume as well as the role of networking and informational interviews for marketing the resume. Includes worksheets, examples of effective resumes and letters, and a bibliography. Popular with career counselors, students, and adults who can use it as a broader career planning and job search book.

Parker, Yana, *The Damn Good Resume Guide* (Berkeley, CA: Ten Speed Press, 1986, $6.95). A brief irreverent look at how to write a resume with emphasis of the language of skills and accomplishments. Includes numerous useful resume writing tips, 22 resume examples, a few cover letters, and a question-answer section. Most examples follow the author's preference for a "Highlights of Qualifications" or "Summary of Qualifications" section positioned immediately after a brief objective statement. Most resume examples follow the functional or combination format.

Parker, Yana, *The Resume Catalog: 200 Damn Good Examples* (Berkeley, CA: Ten Speed Press, 1988, $13.95). As the subtitle suggests, this is primarily a resume example book. Similar to the examples presented in the author's other book, the examples here follow the "Summary of Qualifications" pattern. Most are developed around the functional and combination formats. Includes few chronological resumes. One of the best resume example books available—a rich resource for anyone wishing to examine resumes written for a variety of positions and occupational fields using functional language and including numerous examples of the "Summary of Qualifications" section.

Schuman, Nancy and William Lewis, *Revising Your Resume* (New York: Wiley, 1987, $13.95). A helpful guide to the principles of resume writing and revising. Organized around a series of 60 "Rules" each of which are explained in a paragraph or two and sometimes in a page or two; some include examples to illustrate the rules. Includes 17 "model resumes" that more or less follow "The Rules." However, only five examples include an "Objective" and these are all self-centered rather than employer-centered.

Swanson, David, ***The Resume Solution: How To Write (And Use) a Resume That Gets Results*** (Indianapolis, IN: JIST Works, 1991, $10.95). This is one of the more complete resume writing and production guides. Gives sound advice on how to write each resume section, including worksheets for generating data. Includes sample resumes and cover letters. Despite the subtitle, the book does not tell how to use the resume in terms of distribution and follow-up. It only takes the resume to the print shop, and follow-up is limited to writing "thank you" letters.

Yate, Martin John, ***Resumes That Knock 'Em Dead*** (Holbrook, MA: Bob Adams, 1991, $7.95). This popular annually revised resume writing guide outlines standard principles of resume writing and production only. It includes some controversial advice (okay to use the personal pronoun "I") and makes "effectiveness" claims without addressing the critical issues of resume distribution and follow-up that define effectiveness. Includes over 100 resume examples organized by positions and occupations as well as a few resumes for special situations. Examples appear to be compiled from non-author sources and thus not all appear related to the principles. Includes a brief chapter on cover letters. Overall, one of the better resume books on the market today. A computerized system based on this book is also available for IBM and compatible systems: ***The Instant Resume System*** (Lightningword Corporation, 1601 Civic Center Dr., Suite 206, Santa Clara, CA 95050, Tel. 408/241-1990, $49.95).

COMPUTER SOFTWARE PROGRAMS

While you can easily produce a resume on standard word processing programs, such as WordPerfect, WordStar, or Multimate, several computer software programs are now specially designed for generating resumes in different formats. All you need to do is enter your data for each information category, and the program will do the rest. Keep in mind that these programs will not write the resume for you. You still need to know how to write each section of your resume. They merely make the layout and data management tasks easier. They are designed to produce a professional looking resume. Most programs designed for individual use sell for $49.95. Some multi-user programs cost more the $100, with some versions costing nearly $1,000.

You will find numerous resume software programs available at your local computer software store or through direct-mail catalogs. Some programs are not much better than a standard word proccessing program whereas others are powerful resume building tools, complete with "canned" resume language and cover letter capabilities. Some of the most popular resume software programs include the following:

The Creative Resume (Educational Associates, 8 Crab Orchard Road, Frankfort, KY 40602, $139.95). Available for both IBM and Apple computers. Designed for teaching students basic resume writing skills. Includes several sample resume formats. Enables user to develop own custom-designed resume.

The Instant Resume System (Lightningword Corporation, 1601 Civic Center Dr., Suite 206, Santa Clara, CA 95050, $49.95). Based on John Martin Yate's *Resumes That Knock 'Em Dead*, this program is designed to produce professional quality resumes and letters. Includes 200 resumes.

The Perfect Resume Computer Kit (Permax Systems, Inc., 5008 Gordon Avenue #2, Box 6455, Madison, WI 53615-0455). Based on Tom Jackson's *The Perfect Resume* book and created by Tom Jackson and Bill Buckingham, it consists of two modules—The Career Consultant and The Resume Builder. The first module includes over 300 words and expressions to use on a resume and recommends best resume format to use. The second module custom tailors, changes emphasis and formats, and gives advice and tips. Available in four different versions: personal ($49.95), Counselor's ($259.95), Lab Pack ($639.95), and Network ($995.95).

The Right Resume Writer I and II (Career Development Software, 2051 SE Columbia Way, Vancouver, WA 98661). Used widely in schools throughout the country, these two programs are available for both IBM and Apple computers. *The Right Resume Writer I* ($59.95) is designed for beginning and intermediate resume writers. It includes three resume formats and has special print features for saving/retrieving resumes and automatic formatting of unlimited resumes. *The Right Resume Writer II* ($102.95) is designed for more advanced resume writers. Includes four different types of resumes and ten preformatted inputs.

The Resume Kit (Spinnaker Software, 1 Kendall Square, Cambridge, MA 02139). Designed for IBMs and compatibles. Offers nine resume formats, spell check, and layout and font options.

Re$ume! (North American InfoNet, P.O. Box 750008, Petaluma, CA 94975. Designed for IBMs and compatibles and Macintosh computers. Offers three resume formats and a list of skills from which to develop your resume language.

ResumeMaker (Individual Software, Inc., 125 Shoreway Rd., #3000, San Carlos, CA 94070). Designed for IBMs and compatibles. Offers three resume formats. Includes spell checker and mail merge, library, activities log, appointment calendar, and "canned" job search letters.

RESUME VIDEOS

Several videos also assist resume writers in developing effective resume writing skills. Three such programs include

Does Your Resume Wear Blue Jeans? Resume Writing Workshop (Blue Jeans Press, P.O. Box 5628, Charlottesville, VA 22905, $129.95). Created by the author of the book *Does Your Resume Wear Blue Jeans?*, C. Edward Good, this 2-tape workshop program of nearly two hours covers all the basics of writing an effective resume. The tapes consist of the author presenting a workshop on resume writing.

The Miracle Resume (JIST Works, 630 N. College Ave., Suite 425, Indianapolis, IN 46202, $99.95). This entertaining 23-minute video offers basic resume writing tips. Explains different types of resumes as well as what should be included in each resume section. Excellent resource for introducing resume writing basics.

The Video Resume Writer (Career Development Software, 2051 SE Columbia Way, Vancouver, WA 98661, $102.95). Designed for all ages, but especially relevant to students, this creatively designed video is set in the time of King Arthur deep in the dungeon laboratory of Merlin the Magician. With the assistance of Egor the Toothless, Merlin uses examples to guide the viewer thorough each section of the resume. Discusses each resume section as well as different resume formats.

JOB SEARCH LETTERS

Resumes are only as good as the cover letters that accompany them. Indeed, many employers report that cover letters are sometimes more important than resumes. While several resume books also include a brief section on cover letters, several other books focus only on writing effective cover letters and other job search letters. These include

Beatty, Richard H., *The Perfect Cover Letter* (New York, NY: Wiley & Sons, 1989, $9.95). Examines all elements in a well constructed cover letter. Includes examples of effective cover letters in the job search.

Frank, William S., *200 Letters For Job Hunters* (Berkeley, CA: Ten Speed Press, 1990, $14.95). Presents 200 examples of job search letters that can be used for nearly any job search occasion. A rich resource for examining letter style and content.

Frank, William S., *Instant Job Winning Letters* (Denver, CO: Career-Lab, 1990, $39.95). Easy-to-use software program (IBM and compatibles) based on the author's book. Includes more than 200 letters that can be used to answer want ads, impress recruiters, break into new companies, make cold calls, arrange interviews, and negotiate salary.

Hansen, Katharine, *Dynamic Cover Letters* (Berkeley, CA: Ten Speed Press, 1990, $6.95). Outlines the basic elements for producing effective cover letters. Includes several examples which are graded according to their quality.

Krannich, Ronald L. and Caryl Rae Krannich, *Dynamite Cover Letters* (Woodbridge, VA: Impact Publications, 1992, $9.95). Covers the basics of writing, producing, distributing, following-up, and evaluating cover letters and other written job search communication. Includes examples that follow the principles of effective letter writing.

Krannich, Ronald L. and Caryl Rae Krannich, *Job Search Letters That Get Results: 201 Great Examples!* (Woodbridge, VA: Impact Publications, 1992, $12.95). Based on the principles developed in *Dynamite Cover Letters,* this book includes 201 examples of job search letters to be written for all types of job search occasions—cover, approach, thank-you, rejection, withdrawal, and acceptance.

Yate, Martin, *Cover Letters That Knock 'Em Dead* (Holbrook, MA: Bob Adams, Inc., 1992, $7.95). Includes tips on how to write effective cover letters as well as numerous examples of such letters.

Appendix

RESUME WORKSHEETS

The following worksheets are designed to help you systematically generate a complete data-base on yourself for writing each resume section. We recommend completing the forms **before** writing your resume. You will be in the strongest position to write each resume section after you document, analyze, and synthesize different types of data on yourself based on these forms. Each form will assist you in specifying your accomplishments and generating the proper resume language. Since you are likely to have more experience/education than the number of worksheets provided here, make several copies of these worksheets if necessary to complete the exercises.

Try to complete each form as thoroughly as possible. While you will not include all the information on your resume, you will at least have a rich data-base from which to write each resume section. Our general rule is to go for volume—generate as much detailed information on yourself as possible. Condense it later when writing and editing each resume section.

The final worksheet focuses on detailing your **achievements**. In many respects, this may be the most important worksheet of all. After you complete the other worksheets, try to identify your seven most important achievements. The language generated here will be important to both writing your resume and handling the critical job interview. You should be well prepared to clearly communicate your qualifications to potential employers!

EMPLOYMENT EXPERIENCE WORKSHEET

1. Name of employer: _____

2. Address: _____

    _____

3. Inclusive dates of employment: From _____ to _____.

                                                       month/year   month/year

4. Type of organization: _____

5. Size of organization/approximate number of employees: _____

6. Approximate annual sales volume or annual budget: _____

7. Position held: _____

8. Earnings per month/year: (not to appear on resume) _____

9. Responsibilities/duties: _____

    _____

    _____

    _____

    _____

10. Achievements or significant contributions: _____

    _____

    _____

    _____

    _____

    _____

11. Demonstrated skills and abilities: _____

    _____

    _____

    _____

12. Reason(s) for leaving: _____

    _____

MILITARY EXPERIENCE WORKSHEET

1. Service: _____

2. Rank: _____

3. Inclusive dates: From _____ to _____.

                          month/year   month/year

4. Responsibilities/duties: _____

_____

_____

_____

_____

_____

5. Significant contributions/achievements: _____

_____

_____

_____

_____

_____

_____

_____

6. Demonstrated skills and abilities: _____

_____

_____

_____

_____

_____

_____

_____

7. Reserve status: _____

EDUCATIONAL DATA

1. Institution: _____

2. Address: _____

   _____

3. Inclusive dates: From _____ to _____.
                                    month/year   month/year

4. Degree or years completed: _____

5. Major(s): _____ Minor(s): _____

6. Education highlights: _____

   _____

   _____

   _____

7. Student activities: _____

   _____

   _____

   _____

8. Demonstrated abilities and skills: _____

   _____

   _____

   _____

9. Significant contributions/achievements: _____

   _____

   _____

   _____

10. Special training courses: _____

    _____

    _____

11. G.P.A.: _____ (on _____ index)

COMMUNITY/CIVIC/
VOLUNTEER EXPERIENCE

1. Name and address of organization/group: _____

   _____

   _____

   _____

2. Inclusive dates: From _____ to _____ .

                       month/year   month/year

3. Offices held/nature of involvement: _____

   _____

   _____

   _____

   _____

   _____

   _____

4. Significant contributions/achievements/projects: _____

   _____

   _____

   _____

   _____

   _____

5. Demonstrated skills and abilities: _____

   _____

   _____

   _____

   _____

   _____

ADDITIONAL INFORMATION

1. Professional memberships and status:

    a. _____

    b. _____

    c. _____

    d. _____

    e. _____

    f. _____

2. Licenses/certifications:

    a. _____

    b. _____

    c. _____

    d. _____

3. Expected salary range: $ _____ to $ _____ (but do not include this on your resume)

4. Acceptable amount of on-the-job travel: _____ days per month.

5. Areas of acceptable relocation:

    a. _____ c. _____

    b. _____ d. _____

6. Date of availability: _____

7. Contacting present employer:

    a. Is he or she aware of your prospective job change? _____

    b. May he or she be contacted at this time? _____

8. References: (name, address, telephone number—not to appear on resume)

    a. _____ b. _____

        _____   _____

        _____   _____

c. _____   d. _____

_____   _____

_____   _____

9. Foreign languages and degree of competency:

a. _____

b. _____

10. Interests and activities: hobbies, avocations, pursuits

a. _____

b. _____

c. _____

d. _____

Circle letter of ones which support your objective.

11. Foreign travel:

	Country	Purpose	Dates
a.	_____	_____	_____
b.	_____	_____	_____
c.	_____	_____	_____
d.	_____	_____	_____
e.	_____	_____	_____

12. Special awards/recognition:

a. _____

b. _____

c. _____

d. _____

13. Special abilities/skills/talents/accomplishments:

a. _____

b. _____

c. _____

d. _____

DETAIL YOUR ACHIEVEMENTS

Definition: An "Achievement" is anything you enjoyed doing, believe you did well, and felt a sense of satisfaction, pride, or accomplishment in doing.

ACHIEVEMENT # __: _____

_____

1. How did I initially become involved? _____

_____

_____

_____

2. What did I do? _____

_____

_____

_____

3. How did I do it? _____

_____

_____

_____

_____

4. What was especially enjoyable about doing it? _____

_____

_____

_____

_____

INDEX

CAREER RESOURCES

Call or write Impact Publications to receive a free copy of their latest comprehensive, illustrated, and annotated catalog of over 1,000 career resources (books, videos, audiocassettes, computer software).

The following career resources are available directly from Impact Publications. Complete this form or list the titles, include postage (see formula at the end), enclose payment, and send your order to:

IMPACT PUBLICATIONS
4580 Sunshine Court
Woodbridge, VA 22192
Tel. 703/361-7300
FAX 703/335-9486

Orders from individuals must be prepaid by check, moneyorder, Visa or MasterCard number. We accept telephone and FAX orders with a Visa or MasterCard number.

Qty.	Titles	Price	TOTAL

RESUMES AND LETTERS

Qty.	Titles	Price	TOTAL
___	200 Letters For Job Hunters	$14.95	___
___	Cover Letters That Knock 'Em Dead	7.95	___
___	Damn Good Resume Guide	6.95	___
___	Does Your Resume Wear Blue Jeans?	7.95	___
___	Dynamic Cover Letters	6.95	___
___	Dynamite Cover Letters	9.95	___
___	Dynamite Resumes	9.95	___
___	High Impact Resumes and Letters	12.95	___
___	Job Search Letters That Get Results (July '92)	12.95	___
___	Perfect Cover Letter	9.95	___
___	Perfect Resume	10.95	___
___	Resume Catalog	13.95	___
___	Resume Solution	10.95	___
___	Resumes That Knock 'Em Dead	7.95	___
___	Revising Your Resume	13.95	___
___	Sure-Hire Resumes	14.95	___
___	Your First Resume	10.95	___

COMPUTER SOFTWARE

____ Creative Resume	139.95 _____
____ Instant Job Winning Letters System	39.95 _____
____ Perfect Resume Computer Kit (Personal)	49.95 _____
____ Right Resume Writer I	59.95 _____
____ Right Resume Writer II	102.95 _____

VIDEOS

____ Does Your Resumes Wear Blue Jeans? Resume Writing Workshop	129.95 _____
____ The Miracle Resume	99.95 _____
____ Video Resume Writer	102.95 _____

JOB SEARCH STRATEGIES AND TACTICS

____ Careering and Re-Careering For the 1990s	13.95 _____
____ Complete Job Search Handbook	12.95 _____
____ Discover the Right Job For You	11.95 _____
____ What Color Is Your Parachute?	12.95 _____

ALTERNATIVE JOBS, CAREERS, AND EMPLOYERS

____ 101 Careers	12.95 _____
____ American Almanac of Jobs and Salaries	15.95 _____
____ Best Jobs For the 1990s and Into the 20th Century	12.95 _____
____ Dictionary of Occupational Titles (1991 ed.)	39.95 _____
____ Directory of Executive Recruiters (annual)	44.95 _____
____ Educator's Guide to Alternative Jobs and Careers	13.95 _____
____ Encyclopedia of Careers and Vocational Guidance	129.95 _____
____ Jobs For People Who Love Travel	12.95 _____
____ Jobs Rated Almanac	14.95 _____
____ New Emerging Careers	14.95 _____
____ Occupational Outlook Handbook (biannual)	16.95 _____

INTERVIEWS, NETWORKING, AND SALARIES

____ Dynamite Answers to Interview Questions	9.95 _____
____ Great Connections: Small Talk & Networking For Businesspeople	11.95 _____
____ How to Get Interviews From Job Ads	16.95 _____
____ Interview For Success	11.95 _____
____ Knock 'Em Dead With Great Answers to Interview Questions	19.95 _____
____ Network Your Way to Job and Career Success	11.95 _____
____ Salary Success	11.95 _____
____ Sweaty Palms	8.95 _____

DRESS, APPEARANCE, AND IMAGE

____ Dress For Success	10.95 _____
____ Dressing Smart	19.95 _____
____ Miss Manners' Guide to the Turn of the Millennium	24.95 _____
____ Professional Image	10.95 _____
____ Women's Dress For Success	8.95 _____

PUBLIC-ORIENTED CAREERS

___	Almanac of American Government Jobs and Careers	14.95 ___
___	Complete Guide to Public Employment	15.95 ___
___	Find a Federal Job Fast!	9.95 ___
___	Good Works	18.00 ___
___	Government Job Finder	14.95 ___
___	How to Get a Federal Job	15.00 ___
___	Jobs and Careers With Nonprofit Organizations	13.95 ___
___	Non-Profits' Job Finder	13.95 ___
___	Profitable Careers in Nonprofits	14.95 ___

INTERNATIONAL AND OVERSEAS JOBS

___	Almanac of International Jobs and Careers	14.95 ___
___	Careers in International Affairs	15.00 ___
___	Complete Guide to International Jobs and Careers	13.95 ___
___	How to Get a Job in Europe	15.95 ___
___	How to Teach Overseas	12.95 ___
___	International Careers	10.95 ___
___	International Jobs	12.95 ___
___	Passport to Overseas Employment	14.95 ___

MILITARY AND SPOUSES

___	Beyond the Uniform	12.95 ___
___	Job Search: Marketing Your Military Experience	14.95 ___
___	Re-Entry	13.95 ___
___	Relocating Spouse's Guide to Employment	12.95 ___
___	Retiring From the Military	22.95 ___
___	Today's Military Wife	14.95 ___
___	Transition to Civilian Life	15.95 ___

STUDENTS AND RECENT GRADUATES

___	College Majors and Careers	15.95 ___
___	How You Really Get Hired	8.95 ___
___	Liberal Arts Jobs	10.95 ___
___	Put Your Degree to Work	9.95 ___

SUBTOTAL   ___

Virginia residents add
4½% sales tax   ___

POSTAGE/HANDLING
($3.00 for first title and 75¢ $3.00
for each additional book) ___

TOTAL ENCLOSED ------------ ___